The Adventures of
Brian

D1341010

The Adventures of
Brian

Eric Thompson

The stories of *The Magic Roundabout*

Originally created by Serge Danot
in a series entitled *Le Manège Enchanté*

BLOOMSBURY

IN THE SAME SERIES

THE ADVENTURES OF DOUGAL
THE ADVENTURES OF ERMINTRUDE
THE ADVENTURES OF DYLAN

First published in 1998

Copyright © by Eric Thompson 1968–1975
Copyright © Serge Danot/AB Productions SA
Licensed by Link Licensing

Bloomsbury Publishing Plc, 38 Soho Square, London, W1V 5DF

A CIP catalogue record for this book is available from the British Library

10 9 8 7 6 5 4 3 2 1

ISBN 0 7475 4242 2

Typeset by Dorchester Typesetting Group Ltd
Printed in Great Britain by Clays Ltd, St Ives plc

These stories are transcripts of the *Magic Roundabout* TV series that appeared on television in the late sixties and early seventies, as narrated and written by Eric Thompson.j32

Brian, Dougal's Friend

Florence was at the Roundabout, waiting for something to happen. And Zebedee was late again.

'Sorry to be late,' he said.

'That's all right,' murmured Florence.

'There's a visitor in the garden,' said Zebedee.

'Oh good,' said Florence.

I wonder who the visitor is, thought Florence, as she wandered through the wood.

And Dougal found out. It was a snail. Dougal and the snail sized each other up.

'Hello,' said the snail.

'Oh hello,' said Dougal. 'Have we met?'

'Don't think so,' said the snail.

'What's your name?' said Dougal.

'Brian,' said the snail.

'Brian!!' said Dougal. 'Snails aren't called Brian. Snails are molluscs.'

'Aren't you funny,' said the snail. 'I like you.'

And he climbed on top of Dougal.

'Shall we go then?' he asked.

Florence was amazed.

'Um. Dougal, you appear to have a snail on your head,' said Florence.

'His name's Brian,' sighed Dougal.

'Hello, Brian,' said Florence.

'Hello,' said Brian.

'Don't encourage him,' said Dougal.

'He's nice and soft,' said the snail. 'I like him.'

'Oh good,' said Florence.

And the snail talked to Florence.

Dougal tried to pretend that the snail wasn't there. 'Looks like rain,' he said.

'It never rains here,' said Florence.

'Sh!!' said Dougal. *'Looks like rain!!'*

'Rain!? I hate rain,' said the snail. 'It's so noisy. I'll be off then.'

And he was gone.

'That's a relief,' said Dougal, 'I thought I was stuck with him.'

'I like your friend,' said Florence.

'I can live without him,' said Dougal, and he went off in a huff.

'Had a good day?' asked Zebedee.

'Yes, thank you,' said Florence.

'Did you meet Brian?' asked Zebedee. 'He's a mollusc, you know.'

'I thought he was a snail,' said Florence.

'Good-night,' said Zebedee.

Cabbages

Florence, carrying a number of parcels, asked Zebedee what snails like to eat.

'I think snails like cabbages best,' said Zebedee.

'Oh good,' said Florence. 'So do I.'

'Really?' said Zebedee.

Florence looked for Dougal and Brian. And there they were.

'Must you follow me about?' asked Dougal.

'You're my friend,' said the snail, following Dougal.

'I was afraid of that,' said Dougal.

'What have you got there, Dougal?' asked Florence.

'What's that, Dougal friend?' asked the snail.

'It's a book,' said Dougal.

'A book, Dougal old mate?' said the snail. 'But dogs can't read, can they?'

'I'll bet they can read as well as snails,' said Dougal. And he left in a huff, which was typical.

Florence wanted to know what sort of book Dougal was reading.

'It's a picture book,' said Dougal, 'with pictures of all sorts of things. All sorts.'

So Florence had a look. And so did the snail.

There is a picture of a cabbage in the book and Brian eats the page.

'Did you see that?' said Dougal. 'He ate a page of my book.'

'He thought it was a cabbage,' said Florence.

'He ate a page! He ate a page!' screamed Dougal.

'You ate a page out of my book,' said Dougal.

'Sorry,' said the snail, 'I thought it was a leaf. Hee! Hee!'

'Very funny, I'm sure,' said Dougal.

'It looked just like a cabbage,' said the snail.

'It was meant to. It was a picture,' said Dougal.

'A picture of what?' said the snail.

'A cabbage,' said Dougal.

'I hope eating that cabbage picture doesn't make you feel ill,' said Florence.

'Funny you should say that,' said the snail (who looked very ill indeed). 'I thought it didn't taste quite right.'

Then Florence said she had a present for both of them.

Some sugar for Dougal.

Dougal unwraps the parcel and gulps down the sugar.

And a cabbage for Brian.

'I couldn't eat another thing,' said Brian.

'I'll keep it for another day then,' said Florence.

'Thank you,' said Brian.

'Not at all,' said Florence.

And Florence told Zebedee all about it.

'I told you snails like cabbage,' he said. 'Snails dote on cabbage.'

And he laughed.

'Time for bed,' he said.

Dougal's Memoirs

Florence told Zebedee that she hadn't seen the birds or the cow or the train recently.

'Haven't you?' said Zebedee. 'Dougal has!'

And he laughed.

Florence asked Dougal what he was doing.

'I'm thinking of writing my memoirs,' said Dougal, darkly.

Dougal looks at his papers.

'And some people had better watch out. Ha! Ha!' said Dougal.

'Secrets will be revealed,' said Dougal.

Two birds fly in to say hello . . .

'Hello, hello,' said the birds.

'Oh, hello,' said Florence. 'I was wondering where you were.'

'We've been for a long walk,' said one of the birds.

'They are funny,' said Dougal. 'I may put them in my memoirs – if I have a spare page.'

And he left.

'Wait for me, Dougal,' said Florence.

But Dougal was busy.

Dougal meets Ermintrude at the gate to the field.

'Hello, Dougal, you dog,' said Ermintrude.
'Good morning, madam,' said Dougal, nervously. And he went on his way.
'Hello, Dougal, you dog,' said a flower.
'Good morning, Miss,' said Dougal.
'Hello, Dougal, you dog,' said the train.
This is getting monotonous, thought Dougal.

The train whistles.

'Er, good morning, train,' said Dougal.
And then Dougal got the feeling that he was being watched. And he was . . . being watched.

Brian is in the tree and Dougal looks up at him, nervously.

'I like you,' said the snail. And he laughed like anything. He laughed so much that he shook the tree.
'Where are you, Dougal?' said Florence.
'Dougal,' called Ermintrude.
'Dougal,' called the train.
'Dougal,' said the snail.
'Where *are* you, Dougal?' said Florence.
'He's lovely,' said the cow.
'He's lovely,' said the train.
'I like him,' said the snail.
'Why is everyone being so nice to you, Dougal?' said Florence.
'They are frightened about what I might say in my memoirs,' said Dougal, darkly. 'The pen is mightier than

the sword. So you can all watch out.'

'We don't know *what* you mean,' they said, and left.

'Where is your pen, Dougal?' said Florence.

'Oh, you!' said Dougal.

And Zebedee came in with a butterfly on his head, which was unusual. And said 'Time for bed,' which wasn't unusual.

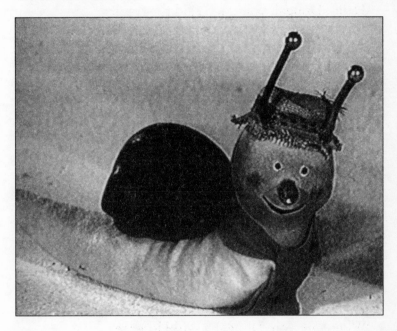

New Horizons

Dougal was thinking . . .

'I must get away from it all,' said Dougal.

'All of what?' said Brian.

'All of you,' said Dougal. 'I want to explore. New sights – new experiences – new horizons.'

'New friends?' said Brian.

'Now we're going to be all hurt, I suppose,' said Dougal.

'I'm not hurt – don't care,' said Brian.

'Don't care was made to care,' said Dougal.

'Well, send us a postcard,' said Brian, crying. 'See if we care!'

'Oh dear,' said Dougal. 'I wonder if Columbus had this trouble. Ah well . . .'

Brian was very unhappy. Who am I going to fight with? he thought.

Brian rushed through the garden telling everyone Dougal was leaving . . .

Meanwhile, Florence was meeting Zebedee.

'Dougal's leaving,' said Zebedee.

'Dougal's *what*?' said Florence.

'Halt!' said Ermintrude.

'I beg your pardon?' said Dougal. 'What's all this? What do you think you've come as?'

'Customs,' said Ermintrude.

Dougal showed his garden passport.

'No good!' said Ermintrude.

'What do you mean no good?' said Dougal.

'Out of date!' said Ermintrude.

'I'll have to get it stamped, I suppose. Really!' said Dougal.

Dougal encountered another snag . . .

Brian drives up in a car.

'What's all this then?' Dougal demanded.

'Customs,' said Brian. 'May I see your passport, please, sir?'

'I'm just going to get it,' said Dougal.

'I shall have to inspect your luggage, sir,' said Brian.

Brian draws a deep breath.

'Ooh . . . can't have this. Can't take sugar out of the country. Ooh . . . this means trouble,' said Brian.

'What *are* you going on about? Great oaf. Hey! Put that back!' said Dougal.

'I shall have to conjugate this, sir,' said Brian.

Dougal felt very thwarted – but try as he might he couldn't get past the customs gate.

Florence arrived.

'Thank goodness,' said Dougal. 'Have you any idea what's going on here – they've all gone crackers . . .'

'Really?' said Florence.

She called to Zebedee . . . and asked him if he could persuade Dougal to stay.

'I might,' said Zebedee, and there was a pile of sugar.

'Oh dear,' said Dougal. 'Er . . . hum . . . No place like home, is there? Take me years to get through this lot . . . Hee! Hee!'

'Dougal, you are dreadful,' said Florence.

'I know,' said Dougal, chortling. 'But look where it gets me.'

Brian's Voice

Florence called to Zebedee . . . who arrived.

'Hello!' said Florence, spinning.

'Hello!' said Zebedee, laughing.

'I feel energetic,' said Florence.

'Do you?!' said Zebedee.

'So what shall I do?' said Florence.

'Go to the garden perhaps?' said Zebedee.

'Yes!' said Florence.

'Thought you might . . .' said Zebedee.

So Florence went.

Dougal was waiting.

'What shall we do?' said Florence.

'Do? Well, do you want to sort some sugar?' said Dougal.

'No, thank you,' said Florence. 'It doesn't appeal.'

Dylan wasn't much help either . . .

'Well, what do you want to do?' said Dougal.

'Don't know,' said Florence.

'Do you want to chase a few snails? Can be fun,' said Dougal.

'No, thank you,' said Florence.

'Music?' said Dougal.

'No,' said Florence.

'Perhaps you'd like me to stand on my head and sing "Annie Laurie",' said Dougal, sarcastically.

'No, I don't think so,' said Florence.

'Well, I wouldn't have anyway,' said Dougal.

'Any other ideas?' said Florence.

'No, I haven't . . . yes! I have. We could pick some pretty witty flowers,' said Dougal.

'What a good idea,' said Florence. 'How clever of you to think of it . . .'

And she leaves, picking flowers as she goes.

Why don't I keep my mouth shut? thought Dougal. Look at me . . . Constance Spry rides again.

'Did you know you've got a mouthful of flowers?' said Brian, laughing.

'I suppose you think that's . . .' said Dougal in a muffled voice.

Dougal takes the flowers out of his mouth.

' . . . funny?' said Dougal.

'Well, it's not something you see every day, is it? A dog with a mouthful of daisies.'

'What are you doing, Brian?' said Florence.

'I am going about my lawful business – spreading joy and delight,' said Brian. 'Old hairy seems a bit upset – what's the matter with him? No one written to him lately?'

'Really, Brian!' said Florence.

Dougal was maintaining his dignity.

'I trust you've stopped hob-nobbing with snails,' he said, leaving.

Meanwhile, in another part of the garden, two willow

trees were doing a bit of weeping . . .

'Oh, woe,' said one.

'Oh, woe,' said the other.

'Oh, woe!' they said.

Brian couldn't stand it . . .

And he retreats into his shell . . .

'Come out,' said Florence.

'Woe!' said the trees.

Florence was worried . . . and so was Dougal and so was Brian.

'It's very sad,' said Florence.

'Well, they shouldn't be weeping willows if they can't stand the strain,' said Dougal.

And this made the trees stop crying . . .

'Down with dogs!' they said.

'What was that?' said Florence.

'They're saying "Down with dogs",' said Brian, innocently.

'Down with dogs,' said a tree. 'Woe! Woe!'

'You really must try to cheer up,' said Florence.

'It's all very well for you,' said the tree.

'I don't know what timber's coming to,' said Brian, as the tree wept buckets.

'Keep away from us,' said the tree to Dougal. 'We want to be alone . . . oh, woe, oh, woe!'

'I wouldn't touch you with a barge pole,' said Dougal.

'Better leave them,' said Florence.

'Well,' said Brian, 'it takes all sorts to make the world, as my old dad always says whenever he gets the chance – which is too often for my liking . . .'

The trees wept on . . .

'It's been a funny sort of day,' said Dougal.

Dougal's Experiment

Mr Rusty was looking at the moon through his telescope.

'Looks quite close,' he said.

'What are you looking at?' said Florence.

'The moon,' said Mr Rusty. 'I wouldn't mind going there to have a look around. No indeed, I wouldn't mind going there.'

'I don't wish to stifle the spirit of enterprise,' said Zebedee, 'but it has been done . . .'

'Oh, you!' said Florence.

In the garden, Florence couldn't find Dougal anywhere. So she asked Brian.

'Well,' said Brian, 'far be it from me to tell tales about my old chum, but he does appear to have lost his cool rather . . .'

'Whatever do you mean?' said Florence.

'He's flipped,' said Brian.

'Flipped?' said Florence.

'Don't you understand English?' said Brian. 'I thought I was making myself abundantly clear. Our shaggy friend has gone dotty.'

'Oh,' said Florence, 'is that all? I thought it was something serious.'

Brian laughed. 'He's over here. Of course, I'm only joking really.'

'I know,' said Florence.

Dougal did appear to be up to something unusual to say the least.

'Now let me see, the square on the hypotenuse equals the volume of Archimedes minus the square root of Pythagoras which gives us a grand total of seven and a half except on Thursdays, which have thirty-one . . . yes.'

'What are you doing, Dougal?' asked Florence.

'Isn't it obvious?' said Dougal.

'No,' said Brian.

'Nothing's obvious to *you*, great oaf,' said Dougal. 'I don't suppose you could even spell "geometry" . . . which is what I am concerning myself with at the moment. I am conducting an experiment in dimensions . . .'

'Of the moon?' said Florence.

'Moon? Who cares about the moon? This is to do with the exact sizing of a lump of sugar,' said Dougal. 'How did the moon get into this?'

'Very important work,' said Brian.

'Yes, it *is*,' said Dougal, 'so I'll trouble you . . .'

Dougal gulps . . .

'Ooh! Swallowed me chalk!' said Dougal.

Florence had a look around . . .

'I'm very impressed,' said Brian.

'Now let me get on,' said Dougal. 'I'm sure Isaac Newton didn't have snails bothering him . . .'

'Who's Isaac Newton?' said Brian. 'Did he invent sugar?'

But Dougal was too busy experimenting to reply . . .

Dougal writes and mutters, scientifically.

'What's all this then?' said Brian.

'I can see all my results *ruined* with you two,' said Dougal.

'Three foot ten,' said Florence.

'Thank you,' said Dougal. 'Now, three foot ten by . . . Three foot ten!? Didn't know I'd got sugar *that* size.'

'No. I'm three foot ten,' said Florence.

'Back to the drawing-board, old thing,' said Brian, laughing. 'And don't add in the date.'

'In spite of interruptions,' said Dougal, icily, 'I have reached an answer . . . and that's it . . . three is the answer. Eureka!'

'Eureka?' said Florence.

'Eureka?' said Brian.

'A cube is a cube is a cube is a cube,' said Dougal.

The Black Flower

Mr Rusty was reading a book when Florence arrived.

'Hello,' she said, loudly.

'I can hear you. I'm only reading – I'm not asleep,' said Mr Rusty.

'Sorry!' said Florence.

'Very interesting book that,' said Mr Rusty. 'All about a black primrose – ever seen one?'

'Never,' said Florence.

'Neither have I,' said Mr Rusty, 'but it must exist – says so in the book.'

'Then it must,' said Florence.

'Stands to reason – must be a black primrose somewhere,' said Mr Rusty.

'Well, I'm not sure that your reasoning is absolutely sound,' said Florence.

Zebedee arrived. 'Problems?' he asked.

'It's just that Mr Rusty wants a black primrose,' said Florence.

'Not if it's any bother,' said Mr Rusty.

'Oh, it won't be any bother,' said Florence.

Dougal is singing to himself. He sees Florence and coughs with embarrassment.

'Sorry!' said Dougal.

'That was lovely, Dougal,' said Florence.

'Woke me up,' said Brian.

'Now I have a problem,' said Florence, 'and I need your help.'

'Naturally,' said Dougal.

'Mr Rusty wants a black primrose and he's asked me to find one,' said Florence.

'I knew it! I knew it!' said Dougal.

'He knew it! He knew it! Shaggy Sherlock,' said Brian.

'Ignore him,' said Dougal.

'Now, what about it?' said Florence.

'What? Oh, this black primrose thing . . . ah yes . . . yes . . . well,' said Dougal.

'Can you help?' said Florence.

'Have I ever failed you?' said Dougal. 'Answer me *that*.'

'I'd rather not,' said Florence.

'Isn't it past your bed-time?' said Dougal to Brian, laughing.

'HAIRY!' said Brian.

'What? What did you say? What?' said Dougal.

'Nothing,' said Brian.

'I've been too lenient with that snail of late . . . he's getting ideas above his station . . . I may strike!' said Dougal.

Florence tried to keep Dougal's mind on the subject of black primroses.

'I hope you're looking, Dougal,' she said.

'My eyes are glued,' said Dougal, 'to the barren ground.'

'Oh, you!' said Florence.

Then she had a sudden thought.

'I've had a sudden thought,' she said. 'Perhaps they

grow on trees . . . In which case we'll need a ladder.'

Fortunately, there was a ladder to hand, and Dougal lifts it up on to his head . . .

'Better humour her, I suppose,' said Dougal. 'Enjoying it, are you?'

'*I* am,' said Florence.

They came to a likely tree . . .

'This is ridiculous,' said Dougal.

But it wasn't . . . because there was the flower. Dougal had some sugar for strength.

'You don't, of course, expect me to go up there?' said Dougal.

'Well yes, I do,' said Florence.

So Dougal went up.

'I shall want danger money, you know?' said Dougal. 'This is madness . . . madness.'

Meanwhile, Brian had found a black flower of his own.

'What . . . what . . . what . . . what?' Dougal called down.

'Yes, what?' said Florence.

'I thought you wanted a black primrose, so I made you one . . . out of lettuce,' said Brian.

'Oaf!' said Dougal.

'Well, if that's the way you feel, I'll eat it,' said Brian.

'My nerves are a jangle,' said Dougal, starting to descend. 'A jangle – I may never recover . . .'

'Careful,' said Florence, holding the ladder.

'Now she tells me,' said Dougal.

Dougal drops the flower.

Florence picked up the flower and they took it to show Mr MacHenry.

'Look what we've got,' said Florence.

'Ah, I'll put it with the others,' said Mr MacHenry.

'Others?' they said.

'Yes,' said Mr MacHenry. 'Flowers get lonely up trees – like people.'

The Oyster

Mr Rusty is playing the barrel-organ.

'Nice,' said Florence.

'Thank you,' said Mr Rusty. 'Exhausting, though,' he said. 'I may have to fit a motor.'

'It wouldn't sound the same,' said Florence, doing a little dance.

'Do you like my little dance?' she said, doing it again.

'I think it's very moving,' said Mr Rusty. 'It brings tears to my eyes.'

Zebedee arrived . . . 'What are you doing?' he said.

'A little dance,' said Florence and Mr Rusty.

'Sorry I missed it,' said Zebedee.

In the garden, Florence called to Dougal, who wasn't there. Brian was . . .

'I am shattered and destroyed,' he said.

'Why!?' said Florence.

'Why? I'll tell you why,' said Brian. 'My shaggy chum has deserted me for another . . .'

'Another snail?' said Florence.

'No, no, no! Worse than that!' said Brian.

'What?' said Florence.

'I thought I was his only shelly friend . . . I was wrong . . .' said Brian.

'Brian,' said Florence, 'you must take a grip on yourself and tell me *all*.'

'I will tell you *all*,' said Brian. 'It's an *oyster*, a common oyster with a knobbly shell, and old shaggy breeks thinks it's lovely and talks to it all day . . . great clump. I've never known anything like it in all my puff . . .'

Brian was speaking nothing but the truth . . . Dougal had an oyster.

'You see!' said Brian.

'Look out, Angus,' said Dougal.

'Ah, company!' said the oyster.

'Common mollusc!' said Brian.

'He can talk!' said Dougal.

'So can I!' said the oyster.

Florence was quite overcome by the complication of it all.

'I've lost my pearl!' said the oyster.

'He's lost his pearl,' said Dougal. 'Nobody leaves the garden. Find the pearl . . . everybody look!'

Florence called Zebedee – who came.

'Trouble?' he said.

'I've lost my pearl,' said the oyster.

'Oh dear,' said Zebedee, 'that will never do.'

Just then, a pearl appears, surprisingly . . .

'Is this it? Looks like a pearl,' said Zebedee.

'My pearl,' said the oyster. 'Come home.'

The pearl goes and Florence gives chase.

'Haven't you done enough gallivanting around? Return to Angus,' said Dougal.

But the pearl hadn't and seemingly didn't want to.

'Ungrateful thing,' said Dougal.

'Hello, pearl,' said Brian.

'Got it?' said Florence.

Brian curls and uncurls as the pearl nips into his shell . . .

'No stop that! Stop it!' said Brian, laughing.

'Now pearl,' said Florence, 'you're in the wrong shell.'

'He'll sell you,' said Dougal, with a laugh, 'if you don't come out.'

'What shall we do?' said Florence.

'Don't worry, Angus,' said Dougal, to the oyster.

Florence called again . . . and Zebedee came back.

'Yes?' said Zebedee.

And Florence explained the pearl was lost again.

'Well,' said Zebedee, 'you'd better find it, hadn't you?'

'Yes,' said Florence.

'Why don't you go back to Colchester?' said Brian to the oyster.

'Whitstable,' said the oyster.

'I'll see you later!' said Dougal to Brian.

'Fair weather friend,' said Brian, leaving.

Dougal looks at the oyster and . . .

'Umm!! Quite tasty!' said Dougal.

Dougal's Jam

Dougal had been making some jam.

'An old recipe of me Auntie Megsie . . .'

The jam moves.

It was a rather powerful recipe.

'Now don't get carried away, you lot . . . I'll be back,' said Dougal.

The jam was disgusted.

'He's forgotten the sugar,' they hissed, quite beside themselves with concern.

'Hope I haven't forgotten anything,' said Dougal.

'The sugar!' they shouted, but being jam they couldn't shout very loud.

'Quiet please!' said Dougal. 'Noisy lot, aren't you?'

'I wonder if I should bake some bread?' said Dougal. 'I suppose *people* will ask me for some, being famed as I am . . . for me jam-making.'

People were arriving . . .

'Hello, Dougal,' said Florence.

'I suppose you've *heard*,' said Dougal.

'No,' said Florence. 'What?'

'That I've made some of my famous jam,' said Dougal. 'Sought after by royalty and known to drive jam gourmets mad . . . um?'

'I'm a jam gourmet,' said Florence. 'Show me.'

'Here it is,' said Dougal . . . but it wasn't. 'What!?
What!? What?!'

'Has it gone?' said Florence.

'That is the unnecessary remark of the century,' said
Dougal. 'Of course it's gone . . .'

Dougal sniffs suspiciously.

'I smell a snail . . . there's a snaily smell,' said Dougal.

'He *wouldn't*,' said Florence.

'You have a touching faith in mollusc nature,' said
Dougal. 'Of course he would! Come.'

So Florence went.

'If I catch him,' said Dougal, 'he'll smart for this . . .'

They encountered Ermintrude, busy eating flowers . . .

'Hello, dear things,' she said.

'Have you seen a snail carrying a lot of jam?' said Dougal.

'I haven't,' said Ermintrude, 'but then I might not have noticed, being a silly old thing.'

Dougal thought of asking Dylan but it was unlikely that Dylan would have noticed *anything*.

'Wake up!' said Dougal.

'Yes? Yes? Like . . . er . . . yes?' said Dylan.

'Jam!' said Dougal.

'Seen any?' said Florence.

'Mam,' said Dylan, 'you will forgive me if I don't quite follow you . . . er . . . snore . . .'

'He wouldn't know a pot of jam if it hit him on the head,' said Dougal. 'Come on . . .'

Dougal walks on, then stops suddenly.

'Now who's this?' said Dougal.

'Mr MacHenry,' said Florence.

And it was . . . Dougal asked him if he'd seen any jam or a snail or both, but Mr MacHenry said he hadn't, but then he hadn't been looking too closely, either . . .

'I tend to overlook snails,' he said, wisely.

'You're lucky,' said Dougal.

'Now don't worry,' said Florence. 'It'll turn up . . . eventually.'

And eventually, to the sound of a tooting train, they see Brian approaching. Laden down with jam.

Dougal controlled himself with difficulty . . .

'Look what I found!' said Brian.

Oh dear, thought Florence.

'It was just lying there and I found it, I found it!' said Brian.

Dougal had a quick count . . .

'One, two, three, four, five, six . . . Come here you!' he said.

'I am a jam-finder,' said Brian.

Dougal retained an icy calm . . .

'All's well that ends well,' said Florence.

'It's *my* jam,' said Dougal.

'Oh, I didn't know that, old jam-owner,' said Brian. 'Your talent is exceeded only by your personal beauty . . .' he shouts.

Brian laughs as he goes into his shell.

Penelope is Lazy

Dougal was in a state. 'I'm in a state,' he said.

'May one ask why?' said Brian.

And Dougal explained that Florence had knitted him a kilt and he'd lost it.

'It'll look so ungrateful not to have it on,' he said.

'Say it's in the wash,' said Brian.

'I suppose we are going to be treated to a lot of very stupid suggestions,' said Dougal. 'I'll trouble you to try and be constructive . . . if possible.'

'I am constructive,' said Brian.

'No, you're *not*,' said Dougal. 'You're about as constructive as an atom bomb . . . and you look a bit like one too . . .'

Meanwhile, Florence waited . . .

'Waiting for me?' said Zebedee. 'Am I late?'

'Not at all,' said Florence, 'or, anyway, only a little.'

Florence called to Dougal.

'Hello!' said Dougal. 'Isn't it a lovely day . . . ? Yes . . . lovely . . . much too hot to have anything, er, extra on.'

'Like a kilt,' said Brian.

'What did you say, Brian?' said Florence.

'Nothing! He said nothing . . . don't listen to him . . . Ha! Ha!' said Dougal.

'No, I didn't say anything,' said Brian.

'Yes you did,' said Florence.

'Did I? Well, I . . . I can't remember,' said Brian.

'I'll pulverise that snail before I'm through . . . Any-one want a flower?' said Dougal.

'I don't *think* I said anything,' said Brian, with a laugh.

'Now what *is* going on?' said Florence.

'Nothing! You wait till I get you home,' said Dougal to Brian.

Brian retreats into his shell.

'Where's your kilt?' said Brian, in a muffled voice.

'Oooh . . . that mollusc!' said Dougal.

Brian comes out of his shell.

'I don't think I said anything,' said Brian, laughing again.

Brian moves off and Florence starts to follow.

Florence was bewildered.

'Don't go with him,' said Dougal. 'He's dotty – touch of the sun.'

'The Dougals are coming. Hurrah! Hurrah!' said Brian.

'What did I tell you?' said Dougal. 'Quite dotty . . .'

'I wish I knew what was going on,' said Florence.

'Knitted any good kilts lately?' said Brian, with a laugh.

They came across a strange scene . . . a train caught in

a spider's web – not something you see every day.

'Now get out, you great monster,' said Penelope, the spider.

'What?' said Dougal. 'What! What! What! What! I recognise *that*!'

It was a piece of his kilt . . .

'Who's responsible for this? Heads will roll . . . the claymores will be brandished,' said Dougal.

'Eek!' said Penelope.

'Madam!' said Dougal. 'I require an answer! Did you unpick my kilt . . . yes or no?'

'Yes, I did,' said Penelope.

'Then I'll trouble you to re-knit it,' said Dougal.

'But it's got a train in it,' said Penelope, 'and knitting

is difficult enough without having a train sitting on your needles . . . if you know what I mean.'

'It was very naughty of you,' said Florence.

'Naughty? It was the act of a vandal,' said Dougal.

Dougal gets into a truck.

'Vandal,' said Dougal. 'Look at me Black Watch tartan . . . like the battle of Bannockburn, which we won incidentally . . .'

'Bravo, Dougal,' said Florence.

'So get knitting,' said Dougal.

'I'm exhausted,' said Penelope.

'Well, get this train out, anyway,' said Dougal.

Penelope decided to make amends by giving Florence a bow for her hair . . .

'Thank you,' said Florence.

'That's all very well,' said Dougal, 'but what about my kilt? It's hung up here like spaghetti . . . *and* it's got a train on it.'

'Cut it,' said Brian.

So Penelope did . . .

'I'm glad *that's* over,' said the train.

Zebedee arrived.

'All well?' he asked. 'Because it's time for bed.'

'Good-night,' said Florence.

Dougal looked at his kilt.

'They'll never believe me in Dundee,' he said.

Brian's Twilight

Florence and Mr Rusty were talking about Zebedee.

'Have you noticed how graceful he is these days?' said Mr Rusty. 'Very, very graceful.'

'It's his new spring,' said Florence. 'Nylon.'

'Whatever next,' said Mr Rusty.

'Don't let me interrupt your discussion,' said Zebedee, gracefully. 'Talking about anything interesting? Hum?'

'No,' said Florence.

'Oh, I thought you were,' said Zebedee.

'Oh, just this and that and the other,' said Mr Rusty, leaving in confusion.

'You're an eavesdropper,' said Florence, severely.

In the garden, she encountered an unusual sight . . . a cow wearing glasses.

'Horn-rims, of course, dear thing,' said Ermintrude, 'and I expect you're wondering why. Well, I was finding it difficult to separate the primroses from the pansies and that's rather important at my age, as they do taste very different.'

'I think they're very chic,' said Florence, 'and useful.'

'Well they'll certainly come in handy for moon-jumping,' said Ermintrude, hopefully.

'Yes, they will,' said Florence.

Dylan appeared, looking rather agitated.

'Is it fair, mam . . . I ask you . . . is it . . . like . . .

justice, mam . . . is it?' said Dylan.

'Is *what*, Dylan?' said Florence.

And Dylan told Florence that Brian had gone into his favourite carrot patch and pulled all his carrots up.

'He wants to make carrot juice because he's going to Australia – overland. Not even flying,' said Dylan. 'I ask you, mam, should I have to subsidise a snail trek . . . is it right? Is it fair? Is it just? Is it honest? Is it healthy?'

'Well, it does seem to be in the interest of research, Dylan,' said Florence.

'Research, mam? How do you mean?' said Dylan.

'Well I don't suppose a snail has gone overland to Australia before,' said Florence.

And Dylan was forced to agree that this was probably

true . . . and that the sacrifice of the carrots was perhaps worthwhile – if only to get rid of Brian to Australia.

'I'll write it off as experience … like … experience,' he said.

'Very wise,' said Florence. 'Experience. We all need it – and we all get it. But we don't all use it.'

'Ooh!' said Dougal. 'What's all this? Standing in the daisies mumbling about experience . . . oooh!!'

'That'll do, Dougal,' said Florence.

Brian arrives.

'Oh, look who's here,' said Dougal. 'Yes?' he said.

'I have come to say goodbye,' said Brian.

'Oh?' said Florence.

'Yes, I am going on a long and dangerous journey . . ."Don't go!" you will say . . .' said Brian.

'Oh no we won't,' said Dougal, laughing.

'I shall ignore that,' said Brian. '"Don't go!" you will say . . .'

'Don't go!' said Florence, dramatically.

'Have you gone quite out of your mind?' hissed Dougal. 'Let him go!'

'My plan is absurdly simple,' said Brian.

'Yes, it would be,' said Dougal, laughing. 'It would be.'

'Tell us about it,' said Florence.

'I shall,' said Brian, 'if you can persuade your shaggy companion to shut up . . .'

'Oooh,' said Dougal.

'I've decided you need me here,' said Brian, 'so I shall stay to bring you comfort and delight, especially dogs.'

Brian laughs.

Voyage D'Affaires

Mr Rusty told Florence that he'd been thinking.

'It's a long time since I went on holiday,' he said.

'Were you thinking of going *now*, then?' said Florence.

'Yes,' said Mr Rusty. 'I, er, can't think where to go, that's all.'

'Well, ask Zebedee,' said Florence. 'He's good at holidays.'

'I heard that,' said Zebedee. 'Go and see Dougal. He's best at holidays.'

'You know,' said Mr Rusty, 'I'm not too sure about the wisdom of this. Look . . .'

'Hello, Dougal,' said Florence.

'Welcome,' said Dougal, 'to the Dougal Travel Service. Holidays arranged. Satisfaction guaranteed.'

'Brian helping?' said Florence.

'Yes,' said Dougal, heavily.

'I certainly am!' said Brian. 'I work out the best way to go with my map and my powerful brain.'

'What map?' said Dougal.

'WOLVERHAMPTON,' said Brian.

'Wolverhampton?' said Florence.

'Lovely place,' said Brian.

'I'm not sure that's where I want to go,' said Mr Rusty.

'I can see we're going to have difficulty with this

client,' said Brian. 'Doesn't want to go to Wolverhampton. That poses problems.'

'I don't want to be difficult,' said Mr Rusty.

'They all say that,' said Brian.

And Dougal explained that everything had been prepared for the Wolverhampton tour – the special luggage was all ready, for instance.

'And the tropical kit,' said Brian. 'Gets very hot in Wolverhampton – especially if you keep your vest on.'

'Well, I don't want to be difficult,' said Mr Rusty, again, 'but I don't want to go.'

'How about Stoke-on-Trent?' said Brian.

'How about *abroad*?' said Florence.

'Abroad?' said Brian. 'Oooh! That's tricky!'

'You don't want to go *abroad*,' said Dougal. 'All those foreigners milling about as though they owned the place.'

'Really, Dougal!' said Florence.

'Well, what's wrong with Britain? I could offer you the Grand Canal, Manchester, or the Doges Palace, Dundee . . .' said Dougal.

'Or the Leaning Tower of West Ham,' said Brian.

But Florence and Mr Rusty weren't interested.

'We'll have to think of something else,' said Brian.

Florence apologised for being difficult.

'That's all right,' said Dougal.

'We really wanted to go somewhere exotic,' they said.

'More exotic than Wolverhampton?' said Dougal.

Brian fetched more travel books while they prepared for an exotic holiday.

'What about China?' said Florence.

Brian and Dougal went quite pale . . .

'China!' said Florence.

'China!' said Mr Rusty.

'The very place!' said Florence.

But Brian and Dougal weren't too sure.

'Can you arrange it?' said Florence and Mr Rusty. 'At once?'

'Quite sure you wouldn't prefer the Hanging Gardens of Leeds?' said Dougal, slowly.

And Mr Rusty and Florence said they were absolutely positive . . .

'China or nothing,' said Florence.

Dougal consulted Brian. 'How do we get them to China?' said Dougal.

'Bicycle?' said Brian.

'That,' said Dougal, 'is a soppy suggestion. It would take *hours*. And anyway – what *are* they going to say in Wolverhampton?'

Not at Home to Snails

Zebedee brought Florence a letter from Dougal.

'From Dougal?' said Florence.

'From Dougal!' said Zebedee.

So Florence read the letter.

'Dear Florence,' it said, 'I have installed a bell at my front door. If you wish to call on me will you please give three short rings and one long ring. Tell Zebedee that if *he* calls he should give three long rings and one short ring. Yours, Dougal.'

'I'll never remember,' said Zebedee.

'It's a bit complicated, isn't it?' said Florence.

But they decided to go and see . . .

Unfortunately, on the way, Florence lost the instructions about Dougal's bell – and she couldn't remember whether to knock or ring.

Oh dear, she thought.

Dougal, meanwhile, was at home, quiet and peaceful . . .

'Hello Dougal, old matey!' said Brian.

'Did you ring?' said Dougal.

'No, I said hello Doug—' said Brian.

'I heard you,' said Dougal, icily. 'But I didn't hear you ring.'

'Ting-a-ling-a-ling?' said Brian, hopefully.

So Dougal decided that he'd better show Brian the bell. So he did . . .

'Can I have a go?' said Brian.

'No, you may *not* have a go,' said Dougal.

'If you want to see me,' he said, 'you will ring the bell *once* – understand? *Once.*'

'What will happen then?' said Brian.

'I shall say "Come in!",' said Dougal.

'What happens if you're not in?' said Brian.

'Then I won't say anything, will I?' said Dougal.

'Well, no, you couldn't say anything if you weren't . . . in . . .'

Dougal gave Brian a withering look . . . and withdrew, leaving Brian alone – with the bell.

The bell rings.

'I shall do that snail an injury one day,' said Dougal. 'Well, I *won't answer.*'

Brian rings again.

'Funny,' said Brian. 'Dougal said if I rang once he'd say "Come in" . . . I'll try again. He must be in because I saw him *go* in. What a funny fellow.'
'Hello, Brian,' said Florence.
'Going to see Dougal?' said Brian.
'Yes,' said Florence.
'He's not in,' said Brian.
'How do you know?' said Florence.
'I rang the bell,' said Brian. 'Look.'

Brian rings the bell.

'I shall keep my temper,' said Dougal. 'That snail can ring all day. I-AM-NOT-IN-TO-SNAILS.'
Brian and Florence wondered where Dougal could be.
'He can't be in,' said Florence.
'No, he can't be,' said Brian.
'Shall we, er, ring the bell a *lot?*' said Florence.
'What a good idea,' said Brian.
So they played a duet on the bell . . . which made Dougal wish he *wasn't* in.
'I shall go MAD,' he moaned.
Meanwhile, back at the bell, Zebedee wanted to know what was going on. So Brian and Florence told him about Dougal and the bell and Dougal not being in and everything. So Zebedee decided to try the bell too –

three long rings and one short ring . . .

'Come in,' said Dougal. 'Come in! Come in! Come in!'

So they all came in . . .

'Did you ring?' said Dougal.

'Zebedee did,' said Brian.

'I heard *him*,' said Dougal.

'We thought you were out,' said Florence.

'Yes, we thought you were out,' said Brian.

'But you're *in*,' said Florence.

'In bed,' said Zebedee.

All Play and No Work

Zebedee asked Florence what she was going to do and Florence told him that she was going to the garden and she was going to make a necklace with some beads she had in her bag.

'Dougal will help me,' she said, firmly.

'Are you sure?' said Zebedee. 'He doesn't like work.'

'It's not work,' said Florence. 'It's pleasure.'

'Dougal won't think so,' said Zebedee, prophetically.

But Florence waited for Dougal – determined he would help her.

I'll ask him nicely, she thought.

'Good morning, Dougal,' she said, brightly. 'You're just in time.'

'In time for what?' said Dougal.

'To help me with my work,' said Florence.

'WORK?!' said Dougal, faintly.

'You'll enjoy it,' said Florence.

That'll be the day, said Dougal to himself.

'Er, I've just remembered,' said Dougal out loud. 'Er, I've got to . . . to see a dog about a man.'

And he escaped . . .

'What an escape!' said Dougal. 'WORK! Me!'

Then he met Brian . . .

'Just in time, comrade Dougal,' said Brian.

'What *can* you mean?' said Dougal.

'To help me water my lettuces,' said Brian, happily.

'You are a funny little thing,' said Dougal.

'So I've been told,' said Brian.

'I'd like to help you, little mollusc,' said Dougal, loftily, 'but we dogs have to conserve our strength, you know.'

'Oh, I know,' said Brian.

And Dougal escaped again . . .

Everybody's *working*! thought Dougal, amazed.

Then he met Mr MacHenry.

'Er . . . excuse me,' said Dougal, 'you're not working, are you?'

'No, I'm playing,' said Mr MacHenry.

'Really?' said Dougal. 'How sensible.'

'I'm playing at blowing up tyres,' said Mr MacHenry.

Dougal thought about it . . .

'Can I have a go?' he said.

'Certainly,' said Mr MacHenry. 'You blow and blow until the tyre is quite hard. It's fun.'

'Is it?' said Dougal.

'Oh yes!' said Mr MacHenry. 'But you mustn't stop – if you stop it spoils the fun.'

And he left – laughing for some reason . . .

'Mustn't stop,' he mumbles. 'Mustn't spoil the fun . . . Ha! Ha! This is better than working . . . Ha! Ha!' said Dougal.

Florence wondered how Dougal was getting on.

'How's Dougal getting on?' she asked, and Mr MacHenry told her.

'I must go and see,' said Florence.

'What fun!' said Dougal, panting rather hard.

'Dougal!' said Florence. 'You *are* working hard.'

'I'm not working,' panted Dougal. 'I'm playing.'

And Florence had a little giggle.

'Want to have a go?' said Dougal.

'I don't think so, thank you,' said Florence.

'Is Dougal working?' said Zebedee.

'Yes,' said Florence. 'He's helping Mr MacHenry blow up his tyre.'

'How kind,' said Zebedee.

I've been tricked, thought Dougal.

'But remember, Dougal,' said Florence, 'that all play and no work makes Dougal a dull dog.'

'Well said,' said Zebedee. 'Bed.'

The Nutcrackers

Florence told Zebedee that she was going to pick some nuts in the garden.

'And Dougal says he will lend me his nutcrackers,' she said.

'You'd better go then,' said Zebedee. 'Hadn't you?'

'Where are they?' mumbled Dougal.

'What you lost, Dougal old haggis?' said Brian.

'My nutcrackers,' said Dougal.

'Going to crack some nuts?' said Brian.

'Oh, no,' said Dougal, 'I'm going fishing . . .'

'With nutcrackers?' said Brian.

'Give me strength,' said Dougal.

'Did you know you've got a mackerel on your head?' said Brian, innocently.

I hope Dougal brings the nutcrackers soon, thought Florence.

And she asked Mr MacHenry if he liked nuts . . . and Mr MacHenry said he doted on nuts, and Florence said he should have one when Dougal came with the nutcrackers.

'DOUGAL?! I'll get *my* nutcrackers,' said Mr Mac-Henry – and he went, leaving Florence, nutting happily.

Dougal hadn't been able to find his nutcrackers, so he and Brian thought they would make some . . .

'Can't be difficult,' said Dougal.

'Have a go,' said Brian.

Meanwhile . . . Luckily for Florence – Mr MacHenry had found *his* nutcrackers. And they worked very well.

Very well . . .

'Don't they look good?' said Florence.

And she offered one to Mr MacHenry. But Mr MacHenry was too interested in his nutcrackers to eat nuts, so Florence said she would go find Dougal and *his* nutcrackers.

'Goodbye then,' said Mr MacHenry.

Dougal and Brian hadn't had much success (with making nutcrackers).

'I'm a bit discouraged,' said Dougal.

'I can imagine,' said Brian.

'They should be easy to make,' said Dougal.

'Perhaps we should go to night-school,' said Brian. 'Back to the drawing board.'

'*You* couldn't get into day-school,' said Dougal.

'Dougal!' said Florence, arriving. 'You're wounded!'

'It's nothing, nothing,' said Dougal, bravely.

'Brian!' said Florence. 'You too?'

'Yes, and it hurts like anything,' said Brian.

'What *have* you been up to?' said Florence.

'Nutcrackers!' said Dougal.

'Yes, nutcrackers,' said Brian.

'We tried to make some,' said Dougal.

'Yes,' said Brian.

'But Mr MacHenry cracked the nuts for me with his machine,' said Florence.

'That makes me feel much better,' said Dougal.

So Florence gave them both some nuts to make them feel better.

'Don't eat nuts in bed,' said Zebedee.

Brian, Cushion-Killer

Florence found Zebedee having a little sleep, which was unusual, and she told him she was going to see Dougal, which wasn't unusual . . .

'I'm going to give him that cushion for his bed,' she said.

'I can testify to its comfort,' said Zebedee.

'Oh, good,' said Florence.

So Florence looked for Dougal to give him the cushion.

'He'll still be in bed, I expect,' she said.

But Florence was wrong.

Dougal hums as he makes his bed.

'Hello, Dougal!' said Florence.

'Ow!! Oh, you gave me quite a turn,' said Dougal.

When Dougal recovered Florence gave him the cushion.

'Oh, you shouldn't have,' gushed Dougal. 'Oh . . . Oh . . . It's . . . Oh . . . How can I? Oh . . . It's *just* what I wanted.'

'I'm glad you like it,' said Florence.

'Can I try it?' said Dougal.

'But you've only just got up,' said Florence. 'I think you should take a run first.'

'RUN!!?' said Dougal. 'RUN?! I'm not a greyhound,

you know!'

'I can see that,' said Florence, smiling.

And they both walk out into the garden.

Brian was looking for Dougal . . . and he found the cushion.

'What have we here?' said Brian to himself. 'A scattered cushion? Dropped, perhaps, from some passing carriage? Hee! Hee!'

He hums, thoughtfully.

'What's this? Feathers? Can some poor feathered friend be trapped in there? Hello inside,' he shouted.

'Don't worry – Brian is here!'

Brian mutters and hums as he empties the cushion.

'It must be awful in there. Must be very small,' muttered Brian.

Meanwhile, in another part of the garden, Dougal had decided he'd had enough exercise for one day.

'Shall we wander back?' he said.

'So you can sit on your cushion, I suppose?' said Florence.

'I might,' said Dougal.

Brian had decided that the feathers had been lost by some bird. Must be a bit cold by now! he thought.

Dougal and Florence arrive.

'Have you seen a very cold bird?' said Brian.

'My cushion!' shrieked Dougal. 'What! What! What! You . . . you . . . cushion-killer!'

'Oh dear!' said Florence.

'I thought a bird had lost its feathers,' said Brian.

'No,' said Florence sadly. 'It was Dougal's feather cushion.'

'Hmm! I've made a slight error then?' said Brian.

'I wish I had a cushion stuffed with snails,' said Dougal.

'I'm sure Brian did it for the best,' said Florence, not at all sure that he had.

'Someone moulting?' said Zebedee.

So Florence told him all about it . . .

'I see,' said Zebedee, thoughtfully.

'I notice that snail has sneaked off,' said Dougal.

So Zebedee decided, as he often did, to do a little magic for the sake of peace . . .

'I can't thank you enough,' said Dougal, sitting down on his refeathered cushion. 'Feather cushions are so sympathetic.'

'Sleep well, Dougal,' said Florence.

'Sleep soft, Florence,' said Zebedee.

Brian and the Poisoned Cabbages

When Zebedee arrived he told Florence that there seemed to be a bit of trouble in the garden.

'Trouble?' said Florence, faintly.

'Better go and see,' said Zebedee.

'All right,' said Florence.

So Florence went to see what the trouble was.

It'll be Dougal, I expect, she thought.

And she was right.

Dougal is in the garden, sniffing suspiciously.

'Are these your cabbages?' said Dougal to Brian.

'All mine, Dougal old matelet,' said Brian, happily. 'I am a very lucky snail.'

'I don't want to worry you,' said Dougal, 'but they don't smell very good.'

'Hello, Dougal, Brian,' said Florence. 'What's that funny smell?'

'It's these *cabbages*,' whispered Dougal. 'It's awful!'

'There's nothing wrong with my cabbages,' said Brian, indignantly.

'No, no, of course not,' said Florence, hastily. 'It's just that they *do* seem to smell a bit . . .'

The train arrives.

'What's that funny smell?' said the train.

'We think it's these *cabbages*,' whispered Florence. 'Could you take them away? Take them to England.'

'England!' said Brian. 'My cabbages to England!?'

'Do you think they'll like them in England?' whispered the train.

'They like *anything* French,' whispered Dougal.

'All right then,' said the train. 'I'll take them to England.'

Dougal and Florence were glad to see the cabbages go.

Dougal takes one last, offended look at the cabbages.

'Pooh!' said Dougal.

Brian wasn't at all pleased.

I hope Brian doesn't *mind*, thought Florence.

But Brian wasn't going to let his cabbages go . . . and when the train went, Brian went too.

'Glad to see the end of that lot,' said Dougal. 'It offended my highly sensitive and pretty nose.'

'I wonder what they'll do with those cabbages in England,' said Florence.

'Boil them, I expect,' said Dougal, prophetically.

Just then Mr MacHenry came along.

'You look worried, Mr MacHenry,' said Florence.

'I *am* worried,' said Mr MacHenry. 'Someone's taken all my poisoned cabbages!'

'*Poisoned* cabbages,' said Florence. 'Poisoned!?'

'I did it to get rid of the slugs,' said Mr MacHenry. 'Horrid things, slugs.'

Dougal looked quite white. 'I think Brian went with

those cabbages,' he said.

'What!' said Mr MacHenry. 'They'll make him *very* ill. *Do* something . . .'

'Dougal, *do* something,' said Florence. 'He's on his way to England.'

'Do something, Dougal,' said Mr MacHenry, and he left in a rush.

'Do something, Dougal,' said Dougal, foolishly. '*Do* something.'

And Mr MacHenry came back with even more of a rush.

'I've brought my poisoned cabbage neutraliser,' he said proudly.

'But the cabbages aren't *here*,' said Florence.

Meanwhile, back on the train . . .

'When are we going to stop?' said Brian. 'I'm hungry.'

'Eat a cabbage,' said the train, 'and don't talk to me while I'm driving.'

'I suppose I might indulge in a *little* one,' said Brian. 'Let me see . . .'

'What are we going to *do*?' said Florence. 'Poor Brian. Poor, poor Brian . . .'

And Mr MacHenry felt very upset. 'It's all my fault,' he mumbled. 'My fault!'

And then Florence had a brilliant idea.

'Zebedee!' she said.

'Zebedee?!' said Mr MacHenry. 'Of course! Where is he!?'

'Here,' said Zebedee. 'Something wrong?'

And Florence told him all about Brian and the poisoned cabbages.

'I go,' said Zebedee. 'Worry not. I go – see how I go.'

And he went . . .

'Hello, Zebedee,' said Brian. 'Have a piece of cabbage.'

'Sorry,' said Zebedee, and he magicked the cabbages away.

'How could you!' said Brian.

'Tell you later,' said Zebedee, doing some more magic.

'Well done, Zebedee,' said Florence. 'You didn't eat any cabbage, did you?'

'No!' wailed Brian. 'I'm so hungry.'

'Come with me, little mollusc,' said Dougal. 'I'll find you a bit of sugar.'

'Good grief,' said Zebedee. 'Bed for all, I think.'

The Smoking Volcano

Florence told Zebedee that she was wondering how Dougal and Brian were getting on.

'Go and see,' said Zebedee.

'Yes, I will,' said Florence.

And Zebedee made sure she arrived safely.

Brian and Dougal were having a chat about smoking.

'It's a disgusting habit,' said Dougal, coughing.

'It'll stunt your growth,' said Dougal, coughing again.

'Got a cough, Dougal old son?' said Brian.

'Why don't you smoke indoors?' said Dougal.

'I *am* indoors,' said Brian.

And Dougal got so angry he took the pipe away from Brian – and quite right too.

'Well, if you're going to be like *that*!' said Brian, and he left.

Now I've hurt his feelings, I suppose, thought Dougal. *Really*, some people . . .

And he went to find Florence.

Dougal is out in the garden, where he finds a volcano, surprisingly.

Whatever next? thought Dougal. A baby mountain. Smoking!? It can't be – I must be seeing things. It can't be.

But it was and Dougal got just a little bit frightened.

'HELP!' he screamed.

Florence was wondering where Dougal could be – when he rushed in, in a state of great agitation.

'Women and children and dogs first,' said Dougal.

'Whatever is the matter, Dougal?' said Florence, calmly.

'Make for the hills,' said Dougal, getting a little confused.

'Why?' said Florence.

So Dougal told her about the volcano and how he was sure it was about to erupt.

'How do you know?' said Florence.

'It's *smoking*,' said Dougal.

'*Smoking*?' said Florence, horrified.

'*Smoking*,' said Dougal.

Just then Mr MacHenry came along and Florence told him about the volcano.

'And it's *smoking*,' hissed Dougal.

'Volcano?' said Mr MacHenry.

'Smoking?' said Mr MacHenry.

'Where?' said Mr MacHenry.

'Dougal will show you,' said Florence.

'No, I won't,' shouted Dougal.

So Mr MacHenry went to see the volcano.

'Hum . . . yes . . . yes . . . hum . . . ha . . . hum . . .' said Mr MacHenry. 'Volcano all right. Stay here. Won't be long.'

'Stay here!' said Dougal. 'He must be mad. I will not allow myself to be covered in red hot ashes.'

But Mr MacHenry came back with a fire extinguisher . . . and went to the volcano . . . and extinguished it.

'All's done!' said Mr MacHenry.

'Fire's out,' said Mr MacHenry.

'Goodbye,' said Mr MacHenry.

So Florence went to have a look – followed, rather nervously, by Dougal.

'Courage, Dougal!' said Dougal (to Dougal).

'*That's* a volcano?' said Florence. 'Looks more like a cream cake.'

'Appearances can be deceptive,' said Dougal.

And just then a very strange thing began to happen . . . 'It's erupting!' said Dougal.

But it wasn't erupting . . .

Brian emerges from the volcano.

'Good evening all,' said Brian (looking a bit green).

'Brian!' said Florence. 'What are you doing in that volcano?'

'It's not a volcano,' said Brian. 'It's where I go to smoke my pipe in peace!'

'Huh!' said Dougal. 'Huh! I hope your tobacco got wet!'

And Florence had to laugh at the thought of Brian being put out by Mr MacHenry.

'What's been going on then?' said Zebedee.

'You'll never believe it,' said Florence. 'So I won't tell you.'

Brian and the Highway Code

Brian was having a little sleep, indoors, and when he woke up he found a notice stuck on his shell.

It said 'No Parking on the Zebra Crossing, signed Dougal.'

No parking?! thought Brian. No Parking?! I wasn't parking – I was sleeping!

So he asked Dougal about it . . .

'You were parked,' said Dougal, 'on a crossing.'

'I wasn't,' said Brian.

'Oh yes, you were,' said Dougal, '*and you still are.*'

'But how can I be parked when I don't have a car?' said Brian.

'For the purposes of the law *you are* a car,' said Dougal. 'A shell counts as a car . . .'

'But it's my *house*,' said Brian.

'That's even worse,' said Dougal. 'A *house* on the road – whatever next?'

'But my house follows me everywhere,' said Brian.

'No good making excuses,' said Dougal.

'I think you're being unreasonable,' said Brian.

'I can't help it if I have to carry my house with me, can I?' he said.

'You could move, couldn't you?' said Dougal.

'But I'm a snail!' said Brian.

'So you *say*,' said Dougal.

But Brian got tired of arguing and went back to sleep.

'Huh!' said Dougal.

Zebedee, too, asked Brian if he knew he was sitting in the middle of the road.

'Yes, I have been told,' said Brian.

And Florence, who was tired of waiting for everyone, decided to go to the garden alone.

Whilst there, she meets Dougal, not entirely surprisingly.

Dougal told Florence all about Brian being parked in the middle of the road.

'It's very dangerous,' he said.

'But he hasn't got a car,' said Florence.

'He parked *himself*,' said Dougal.

And he told Florence about putting a notice on Brian's shell telling him about road safety.

'Road safety *is* important,' mused Florence.

'I suppose it's difficult for snails to understand these things,' said Dougal.

'Well I don't think there's a section on snails in the Highway Code,' said Florence.

'There's a section on parking houses in the middle of the road, I expect,' said Dougal, loftily.

'Poor Brian,' said Florence. 'It must be very difficult carrying his house with him. But there it is – it's nature.'

'Nature? Nature?' said Dougal. 'Dogs don't carry houses.'

'Dogs are different,' said Florence.

'It's just as well,' said Dougal.

Just then Brian came along . . .

'We were just talking about you,' said Florence.

'Were your ears burning?' said Dougal.

'Snails have a hard life,' said Brian, sighing.

'Poor Brian,' said Florence.

'Huh!' said Dougal.

And Zebedee said, to no one's surprise, 'Time for bed.'

The Imposter

Florence is at the Roundabout, watching Zebedee boing about, as he was wont to do.

Florence told Zebedee, when Zebedee stopped still for a moment, that she had been invited for tea with Dougal and Brian.

'What fun,' said Zebedee.

Florence set out for tea – but of course she had no idea what she was letting herself in for.

'We've only got one cup, Dougal old mate,' said Brian.

'Only one cup?!' said Dougal. 'How can we have tea with only one cup?'

'We could take turns,' said Brian. 'Or use straws.'

'I don't think that would be very refined,' said Dougal.

'What do you suggest then, Dougal, with your mighty and powerful brain,' said Brian.

'Oh, I've gone off the whole idea,' said Dougal. 'One cup isn't enough for three and I'm rather particular with whom I share . . .'

'Florence wouldn't mind,' said Brian.

'I wasn't actually thinking of Florence,' said Dougal, significantly.

'What shall we do then?' said Brian.

'I shall leave you to entertain Florence,' said Dougal,

'and get on with *things* I have to do.'

So Dougal left Brian to explain to Florence about the tea party and went on his busy way.

'I've come to tea,' said Florence, brightly. 'Where's Dougal?'

'You mean where's the tea?' said Brian, all confused.

And he tried to explain about there being no cups and Dougal going off and all that.

'I don't know *what* he's doing,' said Brian, wildly.

Dougal is standing before a mirror, with a pair of glasses.

'Only one cup,' Dougal muttered, 'so humiliating.'

Dougal tries on the glasses.

'Oh! . . . Um! . . . Um! . . . Oh!' said Dougal.

'Hello, Dougal,' said Florence, acidly.

'Dougal? Dougal?' said Dougal. 'I'm not Dougal. My name's, er, Reg. Who is this Dougal?'

And he was so embarrassed about his tea party that he couldn't even look at Florence.

'Dougal, who's Dougal?' said Dougal, with a cough.

'Oh, I am sorry,' said Florence. 'I thought you were a friend of mine called Dougal. He invited me to tea, you know, and I was just looking for him.'

'Well, he's not here, is he?' said Dougal.

'I wanted to give him some sugar,' said Florence. 'Dougal just *loves* sugar,' she added, wickedly.

And Dougal just did not know what to do. He wanted the sugar . . . very much.

Finally he said very quietly, 'I'm Dougal.'

'Oh no,' said Florence. 'You're not Dougal. Dougal is much prettier than you.'

'I am! I am!' said Dougal.

'We'll ask Brian,' said Florence.

So they went to ask Brian.

'Is this Dougal?' said Florence to Brian.

'Oh no!' said Brian. 'Dougal is much shaggier than that.' And he laughed a little snail laugh.

'I *am* Dougal. I *am* Dougal,' said Dougal. 'And I'm very pretty and very shaggy and I like sugar!'

So Brian looked at Dougal for a long time.

'Dougal doesn't wear glasses,' he said, finally. 'Dougal has pretty brown speckled eyes.'

'So have I! So have I!' said Dougal, wildly.

'I think you're an imposter,' said Brian and he left, laughing.

'I'm not an imposter – I'm a dog,' said Dougal.

'Have a good tea?' said Zebedee suddenly.

'Yes, thank you,' said Florence.

'Time for bed then,' said Zebedee.

The Snail Patrol

Dougal was feeling very cold.

'Ooooh! Brr!!' said Dougal.

'What's the matter?' said Zebedee.

'I-am-frozen,' said Dougal. 'It's so cold!'

'*I* thought it was quite warm,' said Zebedee.

'Really?' shivered Dougal. 'Lucky you!'

And his teeth chattered so much Zebedee got worried
. . . 'Run around,' he said. 'Take some exercise.' And he
left.

'I've *tried* running around,' said Dougal. 'And it's very
exhausting.'

'Hello, little old shivering mate,' said Brian, warmly.
'Got a cold?'

'There's no need to be so bright,' said Dougal.

'Tell me all about it,' said Brian. 'I'm your friend.'

'I'm *cold*!' said Dougal.

'Tried running about?' said Brian.

'Yes, I have tried running about!' said Dougal, shivering more than ever.

'Try jumping up and down,' said Brian.

'Will you stop suggesting daft things!' said Dougal.

'Sorry, old fractious friend,' said Brian.

Brian coughs, tentatively.

'Er . . . I was cold once,' he said.

'You jumped up and down, I suppose?' said Dougal.

'No, I lit a fire,' said Brian.

'Now, for once, you've had an idea,' said Dougal.

'You just need some sticks and some paper and some coal and some matches,' said Brian.

'Is that *all*?' said Dougal.

And they told Florence all about it and she said she would help make the fire . . .

They all go off to collect some wood.

'Enough?' said Dougal.

'Plenty!' said Brian.

'We'll need some paper,' said Florence.

'It'll need *something* to get this lot going,' said Dougal.

Florence found some paper . . .

'Not today's, is it?' said Dougal.

'Does it matter?' said Florence.

'No, not really,' sighed Dougal.

'Now all we need is some matches,' said Florence.

'I knew there'd be a snag,' said Dougal.

But they went to Dougal's to see if they could find some matches . . . but they couldn't.

'No matches!' said Dougal.

'Try rubbing two sticks together,' said Brian.

'I'll try rubbing two snails together if you're not careful,' said Dougal.

'Don't think that would work,' said Brian.

'Be worth a try though,' said Dougal.

'Don't be like that,' said Brian.

Florence was still busy with the fire . . .

'We'll get you warm somehow, old mate,' said Brian. 'Don't worry.'

And Florence had even found some coal – but still no matches.

'Can you light these, Brian?' she said.

'Of course, I was a boy scout,' said Brian.

'What patrol?' said Dougal.

'The snail patrol,' said Brian.

But Florence thought they'd better ask Zebedee to help . . .

'Try jumping up and down,' said Zebedee.

'Stop saying that!' said Dougal.

So Zebedee did a little magic . . . and produced an electric blanket.

'Better?' said Florence.

'Marvellous!' said Dougal. 'Isn't progress wonderful!'

'But why were you so cold?' said Florence.

'Yes, why?' said Zebedee.

'Well,' said Dougal, 'I saw a bucket of ice and I thought it was sugar and I . . . er . . . Ha! Ha! Fell in . . . hum.'

'Is the blanket plugged in?' hissed Brian.

'Don't tell him, but NO!' said Zebedee. 'Good-night.'

Brian, Brown Owl

Florence asked Zebedee what she should do today.

'Can't you think of anything?' he said.

'No,' said Florence.

'See what turns up then,' said Zebedee.

'All right,' said Florence.

But when Florence got to the garden there was no one and nothing going on.

I wonder where everyone is? she thought.

Dougal and Brian were camping.

'Ah! Reminds me of my scouting days,' said Dougal.

'Were you a Scout?' said Brian.

'I was,' said Dougal.

'I was a Brownie,' said Brian, proudly.

'A *BROWNIE*!?' said Dougal.

'Yes, Dougal old mate. A Brownie!' said Brian.

'You couldn't have been a Brownie,' said Dougal, very slowly and distinctly. 'You-are-not-a-girl.'

'Well, I thought they had a prettier uniform,' said Brian. 'And it was ages before they found out.'

'I don't believe a word of it,' said Dougal.

So they finished putting up the tent.

'Won't Florence get a surprise,' said Dougal. 'A Brownie! Huh.'

There was someone else in the garden too.

Dylan is tuning his guitar and humming, tunefully.

A string breaks.

Dylan looked at the broken string. 'Like, man, I broke a string,' he said.

And so he looked about, as you would, for another one.

Dylan sees a tent string vibrating.

'Music, man, music,' said Dylan, happily. 'Hum, lucky me,' he added, and he took the string – from Dougal's tent.

Meanwhile, Florence had met up with Dougal and Brian.

'Hello! Hello! Hello!' they all said.

'We've, er, got a surprise for you,' said Dougal.

'Big surprise,' said Brian.

'What *is* it?' said Florence.

'You'll see,' said Brian.

'Show the way, Brown Owl,' said Dougal.

'Brown Owl? Who's that?' said Florence.

'He's joking,' said Brian. 'Everyone knows I'm a snail.'

'Oh, come along!' said Dougal.

So Florence went to see the surprise – and she wasn't the only one to get a surprise.

Dylan was strumming quietly, in front of the collapsed tent.

'What's all this?!' said Dougal, loudly.

'Greetings,' said Dylan, playing a few chords. 'Greetings! Greetings!'

But Dougal was not to be greeted – he was furious

about the tent. 'What about the tent!' he said.

'We can put it back up,' said Florence, reasonably.

'Put it back up, man,' said Dylan, dreamily.

'You've taken the *string*,' said Dougal, shortly.

'I *need* the string,' said Dylan.

'He *needs* the string,' said Florence.

'He needs something,' said Dougal, dangerously. 'And he'll get it if he's not careful,' he said, darkly.

'We must think of something,' said Florence.

'We must think of something, man,' said Dylan.

'I've *thought*,' said Dougal. 'Give me the string back.'

But just then Brian arrived with something wrapped round his horns . . .

'What have you got *there*?' said Dougal, slowly.

'Tent rope,' said Brian.

'Oh, Brian, you are clever,' said Florence.

'Am I?' said Brian. 'I just thought it might come in useful, that's all.'

So with Brian's rope they put the tent back up.

'Didn't think he had it *in* him,' said Dougal.

'Didn't think what, Dougal old dog?' said Brian.

'Nothing,' said Dougal.

'Real clever snail,' said Dylan. 'Should go far – succeed in life.'

Florence looked at him.

'Try to be a little more careful in future,' she said, severely. 'And now play us a tune.'

'Mood's gone, man,' said Dylan, 'mood's gone . . .'

And he left.

'Don't hurry back,' said Dougal.

'Ah well,' said Florence, 'all's well that ends well, I suppose.'

And she thanked Dougal and Brian for the surprise and gave Dougal a piece of sugar . . .

'You're lovely, Florence,' said Dougal.

'Bed, man,' said Zebedee.

The Rocking-Chair

Florence told Zebedee that she was feeling a little tired and would just like to take a short, restful walk.

'In the garden?' said Zebedee.

'I think so,' said Florence.

'Good luck then,' said Zebedee.

'Thank you,' said Florence.

Dougal was taking a walk too . . .

He sees a rocking-chair, quite fortuitously.

'A rocking-chair! Just what I've always wanted! Oh, joy and delight!' said Dougal.

But Dougal's joy and delight was short-lived . . .

'Hello!' said Brian.

'Oh, hello,' said Dougal. 'Is, er, that *your* rocking-chair?' he said.

'Yes,' said Brian. 'I found it. It's just what I've always wanted.'

Dougal thought very hard . . . 'Hmm . . .' said Dougal.

'What're you thinking about, old thing?' said Brian.

'Oh, er, nothing . . . nothing,' said Dougal.

'Go on, tell me!' said Brian. 'Go on.'

'Oh, it was just that I was out for a walk and I saw something,' said Dougal with a laugh. 'But you wouldn't be interested.'

'What was it?' said Brian.

'A lettuce,' said Dougal, casually.

'A lettuce?' said Brian, eagerly.

'Yes, a *huge* lettuce – amazing really – must have been nearly as big as you. Really amazing,' said Dougal, laughing. 'Well, I must be off. Goodbye.'

'Wait!' said Brian. 'You haven't told me where it is! *Where is it?*'

'Haven't I? Oh, it's quite close,' said Dougal. 'Why don't you go and see?'

'It does sound very tasty,' said Brian, slowly.

And Dougal thought his plan to get Brian out of the chair had worked but, as he discovered, the best laid plans of mice and dogs sometimes go wrong . . .

'Shall we go then, old lettuce hunter?' said Brian.

'Wait there, rocking-chair – I'll get back soon,' whispered Dougal. 'Come on, nuisance.'

Florence, meanwhile, had had a restful walk . . . and, *she* found the rocking-chair too.

'Oh, just what I've always wanted,' she said, starting to hum a tune.

'Good morning, good morning,' said Mr MacHenry.

'Good morning,' said Florence.

'Is that a rocking-chair?' said Mr MacHenry.

'Yes, it is,' said Florence, rocking.

'Just what I've always wanted,' sighed Mr MacHenry.

'Haven't you got one?' said Florence.

'No,' said Mr MacHenry. 'Er, is that one yours?'

'No,' said Florence. 'I found it. I think it's been abandoned. Would you like it?'

'Well, it's just what I've always wanted,' said Mr MacHenry, wistfully.

So Florence said she thought Mr MacHenry should have the chair – especially as he'd always wanted one.

So he took it.

'I'm *so* happy,' said Mr MacHenry.

'I'm *so* glad,' said Florence.

Dougal, meanwhile, had managed to lose Brian and was hurrying back to his rocking-chair . . .

'Oh, I can't wait! Rock, rock. Rock around the clock. Ho! Ho!'

'Hello, Dougal,' said Florence.

'Hello, Florence,' said Dougal.

'Where is it? Hum . . . where's it gone?' muttered Dougal.

'Lost something, Dougal?' said Florence.

'Um? Oh, no! No! Er, have you, er, been here long?' said Dougal.

And Florence told him that she hadn't been there very long but she'd been for a walk and seen Mr MacHenry and had given him a rocking-chair and . . .

'Wait!' said Dougal. 'A rocking-chair? Ah! I fear the worst!'

'Oh, was it yours?' said Florence.

'In a manner of speaking, yes,' said Dougal.

'I thought it had been abandoned,' said Florence.

'It's just that I'd always wanted one,' sighed Dougal, heavily.

'I'm so sorry,' said Florence, 'but I didn't know.'

And she told Dougal that if he went to see Mr MacHenry, he would be sure to let him have a rock. And Dougal thought this was a good idea.

'He may have some sugar, too,' he said – and went.

And Florence waited to see Zebedee to tell him all about it.

'A rocking-chair?!' he said. 'Just what I've always wanted. Time for bed.'

Hunger Pangs

Dougal was having a little trouble with a tin of fruit he'd acquired . . .

'What you got there, old mate?' said Brian.

'It's a tin,' said Dougal.

'Oh really. I thought it was a bicycle,' said Brian. 'Hee! Hee!'

'Highly witty!' said Dougal. 'But you'd be better employed helping me open it.'

And, when he told Brian it was fruit, Brian was very anxious to open it . . .

'You haven't a tin-opener about you, I suppose,' said Dougal.

'It's funny you should ask that,' said Brian, 'because I *haven't*.'

'Typical!' said Dougal.

'I'm a useless snail,' said Brian, happily.

So Dougal decided that they would have to have outside help with the tin and he thought that Florence would probably have a tin-opener. So they called her . . .

'FLORENCE! FLORENCE! FLORENCE! Yoo! Hoo! FLORENCE! Yoo! Hoo!' they said.

'Someone call?' said Zebedee.

'Florence, you've changed,' said Dougal.

'I'm not Florence,' said Zebedee. 'I'm Zebedee.'

'I'm so sorry,' said Dougal, laughing. 'Hum!'

'You want Florence?' said Zebedee.

Dougal and Brian said they did need Florence so Zebedee said he would get her, which he did.

'Dougal and Brian want you,' said Zebedee.

'I wonder what for?' said Florence.

'Yes, I wonder,' said Zebedee.

So Florence went to see what Dougal and Brian wanted. 'What do you want?' she asked.

'Have you a tin-opener?' said Dougal.

'A *tin-opener*?!' said Florence.

'Just, er, an *ordinary* tin-opener,' said Dougal.

But Florence said she didn't usually carry a tin-opener about with her and she asked Dougal what he wanted it for.

'I want to open a tin,' said Dougal, distinctly.

Brian decided that the conversation wasn't really getting anyone anywhere. 'I think I'll go and get a lettuce before we all starve,' he said.

Dougal was beginning to think that the tin would never be opened. 'Shall I try a hammer?' he said.

'I think that might be a bit dangerous, Dougal,' said Florence.

'What about a saw, then?' said Dougal.

But Florence didn't think that was a good idea, either.

'I have a feeling we're not getting very far,' said Dougal, 'and I'm hungry.'

'Want to try a piece of lettuce to stave off the pangs?' said Brian.

'To *what*?!' said Dougal. 'And you're not being much help, either!!'

'Don't be like that,' said Brian.

Florence thought of Zebedee . . .

'Someone thinking about me?' said Zebedee.

So they asked him if he could help with the problem.

'You need a tin-opener,' said Zebedee.

'Brilliant,' said Dougal. 'A tin-opener.'

'A tin-opener – all right?' said Zebedee, producing a tin-opener.

And Brian and Dougal said thank you very much.

'Don't eat too much before bed,' said Zebedee.

'Tell Dougal – *he's* got the tin,' said Brian, sighing.

Going Underground

Zebedee found the garden rather crowded. Everything seemed to be very busy, including Dougal . . .

'Burying a bone?' said Zebedee.

'Certainly not,' said Dougal. 'A disgusting habit.'

'Oh, I thought all dogs buried bones,' said Zebedee.

'All dogs is not *me*,' said Dougal, with great dignity.

'No, that's true,' said Zebedee, and he left.

And Dougal went on with his digging . . .

'Burying a bone?' said Mr MacHenry.

'Certainly not,' said Dougal. 'A disgusting habit.'

And he decided that as everyone was obviously going to ask him what he was doing, he'd better tell them . . .

'I'm digging an underground railway,' he said, distinctly.

'An underground railway?' said Mr MacHenry with horror. 'But what about my plants? What about the trees? Everything will be disturbed!'

'That's progress, I'm afraid,' said Dougal. 'We live in a machine age. Think of the benefits . . . and the profits.'

But Mr MacHenry couldn't think of the benefits or the profits – he could only think of the flowers and the trees.

Engineers and planners have a difficult time, thought Dougal.

'I will consider your objections,' he said.

'Hello, old mole,' said Brian.

'No, I am *not* burying bones,' said Dougal.

'I didn't think you *were*,' said Brian.

'Oh, didn't you?' said Dougal.

'It's a disgusting habit,' said Brian. 'I think it's an underground railway,' he said.

Dougal looked at him suspiciously. 'How did you know?' he said.

'An inspired guess,' said Brian.

'Well you're right, for once,' said Dougal. 'But I must get on with it, if you'll excuse me . . .'

'Good morning, Dougal,' said Florence, brightly. 'Burying a bone?'

'Certainly not,' said Dougal.

'I'm so glad,' said Florence. 'It's a disgusting habit.'

'It's an underground railway,' said Mr MacHenry, sadly.

'Really?' said Florence.

'Where will it go?' she said.

'I beg your pardon?' said Dougal.

'Where will it go?' said Florence. 'From where . . . to where?'

'Well,' said Dougal, 'you may have noticed it's a bit crowded around here – it will take every*one* and every-*thing* where they want to go. And a very good thing too.'

'I see,' said Florence.

'It'll be a great benefit,' said Dougal. 'Not to speak of the profits.'

'I see,' said Florence.

'Finished the underground?' said Brian, eagerly.

'Not yet,' said Dougal. 'Come back in four years.'

'Four years?!' said Brian. 'I'll be old and grey by then. And I was looking forward to going fast, for once.'

And when Zebedee arrived he said that the underground railway idea should be dropped – or *someone's* feelings would be hurt.

'Always ready – never late,' said the train, coyly.

Brian, Vegetable Specialist

Florence met Zebedee at the Roundabout . . .

'Hello,' she said.

'There's a great search going on in the garden,' said Zebedee.

'Oh?' said Florence. 'Really?'

'Be lucky,' said Zebedee.

Dougal is in the garden, staring at a clover.

'Let me see now . . . 1-2-3, no. 1-2-3, no. 1-2-3, no . . .' said Dougal.

'What you doing, old shaggy?' said Brian.

'I'm counting clover leaves,' said Dougal. 'If you must know.'

'Clover leaves?' said Brian.

'Clover leaves,' said Dougal.

'What's all this 1-2-3 then?' said Brian.

'I want to say 1-2-3-4,' said Dougal.

'Then why don't you?' said Brian.

'Oh dear,' said Dougal. 'I'm trying to find one with four leaves.'

'Is that a worthwhile project?' said Brian.

'Four-leaf clovers are *lucky*,' said Dougal. 'And I can do with some luck with you around.'

'I'll help you,' said Brian, and they both went to look for four-leaf clovers . . .

'1-2-3, no. 1-2-3, no! Is that one? No . . .' said Dougal.

'1-2-3-4, 1-2-3-4, 1-2-3-4. Easy. 1-2-3-4,' said Brian, humming.

'1-2-3. No! Where have they all gone? Just my luck, of course. Entirely surrounded by clover and not a four-leaf one in sight – typical. Typical – typical,' said Dougal.

'1-2-3-4. 1-2-3-4. 1-2-3-4,' said Brian.

Florence asked Brian what he was doing and he told her about Dougal and the four-leaf clover.

'Oh yes?' said Florence.

'Funny, isn't it?' said Brian.

'Yes,' said Florence.

'But he would have one and I said I'd find one being a vegetable specialist,' said Brian.

'Are they easy to find?' said Florence.

'Simple,' said Brian.

And Florence found one.

'Oh,' she said.

'Got four leaves?' said Brian.

Florence counted. 'Yes,' she said.

'I think the difficult ones to find are the three-leaf ones,' said Brian, laughing.

And Florence picked another. 'Shall we go and show Dougal?' she said.

'Won't he be overjoyed?' said Brian.

'1-2-3, no! 1-2-3, no! 1-2. Oh . . . 2s now, typical . . . Oh,' said Dougal.

'I don't think he's found one,' said Brian.

'No, I don't think he has,' said Florence.

'Do you think he's counting right?' said Brian.

And Florence said that perhaps they should give Dougal some of theirs.

'You give them to him,' she said.

'All right,' said Brian, with his mouth full. 'Yoo! Hoo!'

'Yoo! Hoo!' said Brian again.

'What! What? What?' said Dougal. 'What?!'

'Want any four-leaf clovers?' said Brian, laughing.

'I don't believe it,' said Dougal. 'Where did you get those?'

'I found them in the highways and byways,' said Brian. 'For you.'

'I have searched my nose to the bone,' said Dougal.

'Hello, Dougal,' said Florence.

And Dougal presented Florence with a four-leaf clover.

'I've searched everywhere,' he said, 'and finally found one. It's for you – for luck.'

'That's very kind of you,' said Florence.

And Dougal gave one to Brian as well. 'You could do with some luck,' he said.

'I must confess I'm a little confused,' said Brian.

'Four-leaf clovers are *lucky*,' said Florence.

'So take it,' said Dougal, 'and consider yourself lucky.'

'You haven't got a bit of lettuce instead, have you?' said Brian.

'No,' said Florence. And she told Zebedee all about it.

'I know something else that's lucky,' said Zebedee. 'It's lucky I was in time to say "Time for bed", isn't it?'

The Secret

Zebedee thought the children were looking a bit secretive.

'What's going on?' he said.

'Nothing,' said Florence. 'We, er, we're just going visiting.'

'Visiting?' said Zebedee. 'Who?'

'Oh, just Penelope,' said Florence. 'She's making something for you. I mean, us. Hum . . .'

'What did you say?' said Zebedee, casually.

'I said she is making something for us and you're not to ask me about it,' said Florence, getting a bit confused.

'Oh, I don't want to know,' said Zebedee. 'See you later perhaps?'

'Oh yes, of course,' said Florence.

But what they hadn't told Zebedee was that Penelope was weaving a special curtain for Zebedee's house and it was to be a surprise . . .

'Hello, hello, hello,' said Brian. 'Where are you all going?'

And they said they would tell him if he promised he wouldn't tell anyone.

'I'm good at secrets,' said Brian. 'I'll only tell Dougal,' he said.

But they all said very quickly that he mustn't tell Dougal . . .

'Not *Dougal*,' said Florence.

Dougal arrives.

'Someone talking about me?' said Dougal. 'My ears are burning. Am I being – *discussed*?'

But they all said that they wouldn't dream of talking about him behind his back. Wouldn't *dream* of it.

'Very glad to hear it,' said Dougal. 'Shall we go?'

'Go where?' said Brian.

'Anywhere,' said Dougal. 'I'm not fussy.'

'It's a secret,' said Brian.

'What's a secret?' said Dougal.

'Where we're going,' said Brian.

'I think you're keeping something from me,' said Dougal, slowly. 'Am I right?'

So they decided they'd better tell Dougal all about Penelope and Zebedee's curtain or they'd never hear the last of it. So they told him and off they went again . . .

'I don't think I'll come,' said Dougal.

'Oh, it won't be any fun without *you*,' said Brian.

'I suppose you're *right*,' said Dougal. 'Come along.'

But Penelope was in despair. 'Oh woe, woe,' she said, several times.

'We've come to see the curtain,' said Florence.

'Oh woe,' said Penelope.

'Woe?' said Florence.

'I've lost the thread,' said Penelope.

'Lost the thread?' they said.

'So I can't make the curtain,' said Penelope.

'What happened?' said Florence.

And Penelope explained that she was just starting to work when the thread blew away in the wind.

'Oh woe!' she said.

And they all thought it was a bit woeful *and* a great pity.

'Oh woe,' said Brian.

'Don't *you* start,' said Dougal.

But who should arrive just then but Zebedee, all wound up with beautiful silver thread. 'Look what I found,' he said.

And Penelope said it was her thread. 'Thank you very much,' she said.

'Now you can get on with the surprise,' said Florence.

'And no more woe,' said Dougal, laughing.

Tea for Two

Florence was waiting for Zebedee, who arrived, breathless and sorry to be late.

'Sorry I'm late,' he said. 'Been waiting long?'

'No, I've just arrived,' said Florence, sighing.

'Away we go then,' said Zebedee.

'All right,' said Florence.

Florence walks into the garden and looks around, expectantly.

Florence couldn't see anyone but she could hear something in the distance . . .

'It was very kind of you to ask me to tea, old hospitable friend,' said Brian. 'But are you sure we have enough cups?'

'Plenty,' said Dougal. 'Per-lenty.'

'Aren't you having any then?' said Brian. 'Because there's only one cup.'

'Oh dear,' said Dougal. 'What *is* wrong with you? We have two cups – one for you and one for me.'

'I hate to disillusion you, old mate,' said Brian, 'but there's only one . . .'

'Oh dear,' said Dougal, again. 'I suppose this will develop into some futile argument.' He sighed.

'Not if you agree there's only one cup,' said Brian.

'There are two cups,' said Dougal. 'One, two, *two*.'

'It's going to be one of those days,' said Brian.

'I can't think what you mean,' said Dougal.

'Er, have you had your eyes tested lately?' said Brian.

'My eyes are *perfect*,' said Dougal.

'And very pretty,' said Brian, 'but have you had them tested lately?'

'Really, some *people*!' said Dougal – and he left.

'Have I said anything to annoy you?' said Brian, loudly.

'Annoy who?' said Florence.

And Brian explained about Dougal and the one tea cup and how touchy he was.

'There was only one cup and he said there were two – do you think he's trying to drive me dotty?' said Brian. 'It's a thought! Oooh!'

Dougal is looking at the mirror, speculatively.

But Dougal wasn't trying anything of the sort. In fact, he was rather worried about his eyes.

'Let me see, something to protect my 20/20 vision, hum. What have we got?' said Dougal.

He tries on various spectacles.

'What about these? Too much? No, I don't think so,' muttered Dougal.

'Oooh!' said Dougal, with a laugh. 'I don't think I'd get away with it, would I? Why not? Only one tea cup indeed. That snail is just trying to get me worried. Ah! What's that? Oh, it's *me*.'

'Dougal,' said Florence. 'Whatever are you up to?'

'What does it look like?' said Dougal.

'I daren't think,' said Florence.

'Doubt has been cast on the efficiency of my eyes,' said Dougal. 'I am accused of seeing double. Me!! 20/20 Dougal – the first . . .'

'Well, perhaps it was just a trick of the light,' said Florence. 'How many sugar lumps am I holding?'

'Unfortunately only one,' said Dougal.

'That's right,' said Florence. 'So you're not seeing double.'

'I knew it – it's that snail,' said Dougal. 'He's trying to drive me dotty.'

'Perhaps he was just playing a joke,' said Florence.

'He wouldn't dare,' said Dougal.

'Oh, I think he would,' said Florence.

'Then let's,' said Dougal, 'go and sort him out.'

'Sort him out?' said Florence.

'It's a slang phrase,' said Dougal. 'Sorry. Just try these . . .'

Dougal puts on another pair of glasses, as they head off to the garden.

'I understand what you're trying to do,' said Dougal. 'You're trying to make me believe I'm seeing double.'

'No I'm not,' said Brian.

'Oh yes you are,' said Dougal. 'You are, and I'm not and you know I'm not. And, er, you are.' He stopped. 'Where was I?' said Dougal.

'Er, not too sure about our words, are we?' said Brian, with a sinister laugh.

'Now that's enough, Brian,' said Florence. 'You know

Dougal gets easily confused.'

'I know,' said Brian, laughing.

'It's all right, Dougal,' said Florence.

'No it isn't,' said Dougal. 'First it's my eyes and now it's my tongue. I'm cracking up.'

'Nonsense,' said Florence.

And she told Zebedee about it and he said it was nonsense too.

'You're both very kind,' said Dougal.

'You'll feel better in the morning,' said Florence.

'We'll *all* feel better in the morning,' said Zebedee. 'Good-night.'

Letter to the Queen

Dylan was in the garden, alone. It seemed to be a good time to practise a new piece on the guitar, so he made sure his fingers were working all right. They were.

'Like, er, supple,' he said. 'Let's go, instrument . . . One and two and three and four and five . . .'

Dylan sits on a stool and plays.

'Oh man,' said Dylan.

'Awful!' said the stool.

'Er, what was that?' said Dylan.

'Awful!' said the stool.

'Criticism I dig,' said Dylan. 'But this is abuse?'

In another part of the garden, Dougal was dictating a letter to Florence.

'Er, Dear madam, Your Majesty,' said Dougal.

'Dear madam, Your Majesty,' typed Florence.

'Er, Dougal, are you sure that's right? It sounds a bit odd,' said Florence.

'Odd? What do you mean odd? She's the Queen, isn't she? And she's a madam,' said Dougal.

So Florence typed it.

'Dear madam, Your Majesty, Further to my last letter . . .' said Dougal.

'Oh, have you written before?' said Florence. 'Do you often write to the Queen?'

'What you doing?' said Brian.

'I am writing a very important letter to the Queen,' said Dougal.

'Which queen?' said Brian.

'*Which* queen?' said Dougal. 'We've only got *one*.'

'Oh that one,' said Brian. 'I like her.'

'She'll be overwhelmed to hear *that*,' said Dougal.

'Perhaps you'd tell her in your letter,' said Brian.

'I've got better things to write than snaily greetings,' said Dougal, loftily.

'Er, Dougal,' said Florence.

'Now don't keep interrupting while I am trying to write,' said Dougal. 'Now where was I?'

'What are you writing to the Queen about?' said Florence.

'Snails,' said Dougal.

'Snails?' said Florence and Brian.

'Yes,' said Dougal. 'I want to know if she'd like one because if she would, I've got one she can have – very cheap.'

'I shall telephone my lawyer,' said Brian. 'I will not be given away.'

'I'm out of order,' said the telephone, and Dougal sniggered.

'Now, Dougal,' said Florence.

'Yes?' said Dougal, innocently.

'You're not telling the truth,' said Florence.

'Who'd want a snail anyway,' said Dougal.

'Really!' said Florence.

'Well don't get your ribbons in a twist,' said Dougal. 'It was only a joke,' he laughs.

Florence thought they should get on with the letter.

'That was only a joke too,' said Dougal. 'I wouldn't presume to write to Her Majesty.'

'Why?' said Florence.

'Because she's very busy,' said Dougal. 'And she might have me arrested.'

'You're wanted on the phone,' said Brian.

'Tell them I'm not at home – I'm out,' said Dougal.

'But that's not true, you are at home,' said Brian.

'I'm not!' said Dougal.

'Yes, you are!' said Brian.

'I'm not!' said Dougal.

'You are,' said Brian.

'Who is it?' said Florence.

'It's the Queen,' shouted Brian.

Piano Carrier

Florence was in the garden wondering where everyone was.

Where can they all be? she thought.

'I expect you're wondering where everyone is,' said Brian. 'I shall, without any further ado, tell you. Your shaggy friend has a musical problem and he requires help.'

It was true. Dougal was trying to load his piano onto the train.

'Haven't you got any bigger trucks? This one wouldn't hold a thin mouse,' said Dougal.

'Really!' said the train.

Piano? thought Florence.

'If he doesn't hurry up I shall *scream*,' muttered the train. 'What *are* you doing, Dougal?'

'I'm fishing off the end of Brighton Pier,' said Dougal.

'I think he's being sarcastic,' said Brian. 'I think.'

And Florence agreed.

'Doctor Beeching, where are you?' said the train.

'I beg your pardon?' said Florence.

'Nothing. It's just that I would like to remind you that I am a passenger train and I'm not used to carrying freight,' said the train.

'Freight?' said Brian and Dougal.

'We expresses have our pride, you know,' said the train.

Dougal tried to get the rest of his things in, without much success.

'Have you tried British Road Services?' said the train.

'I don't care for your attitude,' said Dougal.

'And I don't care for your piano,' said the train.

'I'll never get to Edinburgh at this rate,' said Dougal.

'Edinburgh?' said Brian and Florence.

'For the Festival,' said Dougal.

'Festival?' said Florence.

'Well, they couldn't get Russ Conway,' said Dougal.

What's *this*? thought Brian.

And Florence said she'd help if Dougal promised to keep calm.

'Gotta keep calm,' said Brian.

'He's about as calm as an elephant stampede,' said the train.

'Now, as I see it,' said Florence, 'we've got to get that piano onto the train.'

'Well, I'm glad we've established *that*,' said the train. 'I was beginning to get worried.'

They pushed . . .

'I've done it!' said Dougal.

'Not quite,' said Florence.

So they pushed some more . . .

'The relief!' said the train.

'All done,' said Florence.

'Anything not in will be left behind,' said the train. 'If I'm any later I'll be blacklisted.'

'What about your whatnot?' said Brian.

'Whatnot I will not carry,' said the train.

'Away you go then,' said Florence.

'The Flying Scot was never like this,' said the train.

'Heigh ho! St George for England and St Pancras for Scotland.'

The Stiff-Necked Heliotropes

Mr MacHenry was worried about his heliotropes.

'Don't seem well,' he said.

So Florence and Dougal said they were going that way and would have a look.

'I've never really *believed* in heliotropes,' said Dougal.

'Oh, why?' said Florence.

'Oh, I don't know,' said Dougal. 'The name, I suppose – can't take them seriously really.'

'Here they are,' said Florence.

'Hm . . . look a bit bent,' said Dougal. 'Do you think they've been got at?'

The flowers did look a little strange and twisted . . .

'I think we've got a problem here,' said Dougal.

'We've got the problem,' said a heliotrope.

'What is it?' said Florence.

And the flowers explained that, being under the trees, it was a bit difficult to get enough sun and they'd all twisted their stalks trying to get out of the shade.

'We were planted wrong,' they complained, 'and we're considering strike action.'

'That should be interesting,' said Dougal.

'It's all very well for you to scoff,' said the heliotrope, 'but I'll bet you wouldn't like to have a bent stalk.'

Florence asked if they could help, and the flower said the only way they *could* help was to get them into the sun – and that was difficult.

'Yes, tricky,' said Florence.

But, as she said to Dougal, something had to be done or the garden would be full of droopy heliotropes and that would be a bit depressing.

'You can say *that* again,' said Dougal. 'Of course we could always dig them up and plant them somewhere else, but then they'd have to be watched and mulched and all that horticultural rubbish. Perhaps we should give Fred Streeter a ring.'

Florence saw Brian and explained the problem to him.

'Well, I don't see the difficulty,' said Brian.

'Ooh! Clever boots,' said Dougal.

Florence asked Brian what he thought they should do.

'Well as I see it,' said Brian, 'you need a bit of sun.'

And they agreed that this was so.

'But how to get it?' said Florence.

'Tell us that!' said Dougal.

'We must catch some,' said Brian.

'Catch some?' said Florence and Dougal.

'Catch some?' shouted the heliotropes.

'Well you've heard of sun-traps, haven't you?' said Brian. 'Come on.'

'I've got a feeling this is going to end in disaster,' said Dougal.

But Penelope, the spider, seemed quite hopeful.

'I'm very good at sun-traps,' she said.

So Florence asked her to trap some for them . . . and she did.

'Show me your droopy heliotropes,' she said. 'All may not be lost.'

Penelope's sun-trap was a great success.

'Does Bert Ford know about this?' said Dougal.

'I don't think we'll tell him,' said Florence. 'He may cry.'

The flowers were very grateful.

'How can we thank you?' they said.

'Send us a postal order,' said Brian, with a laugh.

'I hope we don't get into trouble over this,' said Dougal.

'Why should we?' said Florence.

'Well, we've nicked someone's bright period, haven't we?' said Dougal. 'If it's here it can't be there, can it?'

'Oh no,' said Florence.

'Oh well,' said Dougal.

The Humming Hat

Florence asked Mr Rusty if he was well and Mr Rusty said he was, except that he felt rather tired.

'Come to the garden and have a sleep in the sun,' said Florence.

'That would be nice,' said Mr Rusty.

'Go on then,' said Zebedee.

'Yes, come on,' said Florence.

'How do we go?' said Mr Rusty.

'Like this,' said Zebedee.

'Like this,' said Florence. 'One-two-three.'

And there they were, in the garden.

'This is the life,' said Mr Rusty. 'Just what I need.'

'See you later,' said Florence, and she left.

'Ah, this is the life,' said Mr Rusty, sighing. 'It's so peaceful and sunny and – peaceful,' he says, taking off his hat and going to sleep.

Just then Mr Rusty woke up . . .

As he yawns and stretches, Mr Rusty knocks the hat with his hand.

'Don't do that!' said a muffled voice. 'Don't do that! Don't do that!'

Mr Rusty was quite put out. He didn't know what to make of it all.

'What is it?' whispered Florence. 'What *is* it?'

'I don't know,' whispered Mr Rusty.
'It's your hat,' said Florence.

The hat appears to be humming.

'And it's *humming*,' said Florence.
'I think you're right,' said Mr Rusty.
'It's a moving, humming hat,' said Florence.
'I think you're right,' said Mr Rusty.
But he wasn't right . . .

Just then, Brian appears from under the hat.

'Good morning all,' said the snail.
'Good morning,' said Mr Rusty, retrieving his hat.
'Have we met?' said the snail. 'Do you know my great friend Dougal?'
'Everyone knows Dougal,' said Florence.
'Er, what were you doing in my hat,' said Mr Rusty suddenly.
'He was looking for Dougal,' said Florence and she giggled.
'Dougal's in bed,' said Zebedee, sternly, 'and so should you be.'

Done by Numbers

Florence was waiting for Zebedee and when he came she told him about Mr Rusty and the hat and the snail (and how funny it was).

'Sh! Here he is,' said Zebedee.

'Good morning,' said Mr Rusty. 'Do you know a safe place I can put this?'

'What is it?' said Zebedee.

'It's a parcel,' said Mr Rusty.

'Oh yes, of course,' said Zebedee.

'I'll find somewhere safe for it,' said Florence.

So she went to look for somewhere safe to put Mr Rusty's parcel. And, by a strange coincidence, Dougal and Brian had come across a very safe place.

'What's this then, Dougal old son?' said the snail.

And Dougal explained that it was something called a safe. And you had to use numbers to open it.

Dougal and Brian look into the safe. After conferring, Brian leaves and Dougal decides to investigate the inside of the safe. Brian returns and conscientiously shuts the door of the safe.

I wonder where Dougal is? thought the snail.

And Florence arrived and told Brian that she was looking for a safe place for Mr Rusty's parcel.

'This is a safe place,' said the snail, 'if you can open it.

Dougal did, but he's gone off somewhere. I can't do it myself, of course.'

'Why not?' said Florence.

'No arms,' said the snail.

'Oh, I see,' said Florence.

'It's done by numbers,' said the snail.

'Oh, I see!' said Florence. But she didn't really. But she had a go.

'We need Dougal here really,' said the snail.

But Florence was determined.

Florence tries again and the door opens.

'What kept you?' said Dougal.

'What on earth are you doing in there, Dougal?' said Florence.

'What were you doing in there, Dougal old friend?' said the snail.

'I didn't think that was very funny,' said Dougal quietly. 'I might have been in there for *days*!'

And Florence told Dougal about Mr Rusty's parcel, just to change the subject.

'Was it dark inside?' said the snail.

But Dougal had gone, and when Zebedee came Florence told him all about it. And when she had told him Zebedee said, 'Time for bed.'

It Never Rains

Florence told Zebedee that she was going to pick some flowers.

'I hope it keeps fine for you,' said Zebedee.

Dougal and Brian were having a (friendly) discussion.

'Why don't you go away?' said Dougal.

'I like you,' said Brian.

And the discussion had reached this interesting stage when Florence came along. Which made Dougal and Brian behave a bit better.

'Beautiful day, Brian,' said Dougal.

'Lovely day, Dougal,' said Brian.

'Would you like to help me pick some flowers?' said Florence.

And Dougal and Brian said that they would, er, of course love to help but it looked as though it might rain.

'It never rains here,' said Florence, and she went.

But Florence was wrong. There were some big clouds going across the sun which made it get dark and then light again and then dark.

'Looks like rain,' said the snail.

'What's this, what's this?' said Mr MacHenry.

'We think it might rain,' they said.

'Can't have that!' said Mr MacHenry. 'I haven't planned for rain!'

'I hate rain!' said Brian, who did.

'I love rain,' said Dougal, who didn't.

'What about my flowers?' said Florence.

'Leave it to me,' said Mr MacHenry.

They all wondered what Mr MacHenry would do. They knew it wouldn't be anything *ordinary* . . . and it wasn't.

As they all watch expectantly, Mr MacHenry rakes away the clouds.

'That was devilishly clever,' said Dougal.

'I wonder if the weather forecasters know about this,' said the snail.

'I very much doubt it,' said Dougal.

'All right now?' said Mr MacHenry. 'Bye then.'

So Florence thought she would pick her flowers while Dougal and Brian finished their talk.

'Why don't you go away?' said Dougal.

'I like you,' said Brian.

What a pair they are, thought Florence.

'I like him, I like him,' hummed the snail.

And Zebedee came in to see what was happening . . .

'Time for bed?' asked Florence.

'Time for bed!' said Zebedee.

'I like him, I like him, I like him . . .' said Brian.

The Speaking Tube

Zebedee asked Florence how Dougal was getting on with Brian.

'I'm not sure,' said Florence, slowly. 'I don't think Dougal *appreciates* snails.'

'Snails *are* an acquired taste,' said Zebedee. 'Go and see them.'

So Florence went . . .

But she saw Mr MacHenry first and she tried to ask him about dogs and snails. But Mr MacHenry was being very busy, so Florence went to find Dougal.

Brian is in the garden and, rather unexpectedly, he sees a pipe. As he looks at it, Dougal enters.

'Hello cheeky,' said the snail.

'Please!' said Dougal.

'I like you,' whispered Brian.

'Please!' said Dougal.

'Look what I've found,' said Brian.

Brian looks into the pipe.

'Go down the other end,' he said.

So Dougal went to the other end. 'Anything for a quiet life,' he said.

'Can you hear me, Dougal? One-two-three-four. Testing-testing-testing,' said Brian.

'Testing?' said Dougal. 'He's gone dotty!'

And he listened again . . . and Brian listened.

'What are you doing, Brian?' said Florence.

'I'm talking to DOUGAL!!' shouted Brian. 'Are you there, Dougal matey?'

'Dougal!' called Florence, peering into the pipe.

I'd better not encourage them, thought Dougal, or they'll go on for hours.

'Perhaps he's asleep,' said Florence.

'No I'm not,' shouted Dougal.

Mr MacHenry came along to see what all the noise was about.

'What's all the noise about?' he said.

And they told him about the pipe and talking through it from one end to the other.

And Florence said, 'If you go to the other end and listen, you'll see what we mean.'

Florence calls into the pipe . . .

'Can you hear me, Mr MacHenry?' said Florence.

'Good heavens!' said Mr MacHenry.

'Say something, Mr MacHenry,' said Florence.

And Mr MacHenry said, 'We have discovered a new invention! A speaking tube! We'll be rich! I'll be able to grow orchids!'

'A speaking tube?' said the others.

'A new invention?' they said.

'Too late!' said Zebedee. 'It's been done before!'

'It's called a telephone,' said Florence, sadly.

The Mushroom Identifier

Zebedee asked Florence what she was going to do today.

'I think I'll go to the garden,' said Florence.

'That'll make a change,' said Zebedee.

Florence found something growing in the garden . . .

'Are these mushrooms?' Florence asked Mr MacHenry.

'Don't know,' said Mr MacHenry. 'Eat nothing until I come back.'

So Florence decided to eat nothing until Mr Mac-Henry came back.

Dougal and the snail were talking about mushrooms . . .

'What's this then?' said Dougal.

'Edible fungus,' said Brian.

'*FUNGUS*?!' said Dougal.

'Edible,' said Brian.

'You first then,' said Dougal, smiling a bit.

Mr MacHenry returns with a rather unusual machine.

'What's that?' Florence asked Mr MacHenry.

'It's my mushroom identifier,' said Mr MacHenry. 'Stand back.'

'Did he say mushroom identifier, old Dougal?' said Brian.

'Mushroom identifier! That's right,' said Dougal. '*Mushroom identifier.*'

Brian thought.

'Well?' said Dougal.

'What's identifier mean?' said Brian.

'Don't you know?' said Dougal.

'No, do you?' said Brian.

'Of course,' said Dougal. 'It means, er, it means . . . you get a *mushroom* and you *identify* it!'

'Don't eat anything until Mr MacHenry says so,' said Florence.

'Can't be too careful,' said Mr MacHenry.

'Oh, I don't know,' said Dougal.

'What do you mean, Dougal?' said Mr MacHenry.

'Yes, what do you mean, Dougal?' said Florence.

'What do you mean?' said Mr MacHenry.

'Oh, nothing,' said Dougal, 'except . . . there's a certain snail I wouldn't mind feeding a few mushrooms to. Ho! Ho! Ho!' he whispers.

'Speak up, Dougal old chum,' said the snail, loudly. 'Can't hear you!'

'Shame on you, Dougal,' said Florence.

'Sorry,' said Dougal, looking anything but and trying not to laugh.

And Mr MacHenry took the mushroom off for testing. 'Remember – eat nothing,' he said.

'We'll all starve to death if we have to wait for him,' said Dougal.

'I won't let you starve, Dougal,' said Brian. 'You're my friend and I cherish you.'

'How sweet,' said Florence.

And just then Zebedee came along, with a mushroom on his head. 'I'm a mushroom,' he said.

'Then you won't mind being tested,' said Florence, 'will you?'

A Slipped Spring

Zebedee wasn't feeling very well.

'I've got a stiff neck,' he said. 'I can't put my head straight.'

'Oh dear,' said Florence. 'We must do something about that.'

'I'd be grateful,' said Zebedee.

So Florence went to find help . . . but help wasn't easy to find.

Mr MacHenry rides through the trees.

She told Mr MacHenry . . . when he stopped.

'Did you hear that!?' said Dougal. 'Did you hear that?!'

'Did I hear what, Dougal old mate?' said the snail.

'Zebedee's got a bit twisted,' said Dougal. 'What do you think has happened to him?'

'Well, don't look at me,' said Brian.

'I'm *NOT*!' said Dougal. 'It's the last thing I'd do.'

Florence asked Mr MacHenry if he knew a cure for a stiff neck.

'Not off hand,' said Mr MacHenry.

'We must do something,' said Florence.

'Certainly we must,' said Mr MacHenry. 'We must think, um, um, what about oiling him?'

'I don't think so,' said Florence.

'I think I know a good way to cure a stiff neck,' said Brian.

'All right, Doctor Finlay, let's have it,' said Dougal.

'We *pull* it straight,' said the snail. 'It's probably just a slipped spring.'

'*Pull* it straight?' said Dougal. 'Could you elucidate?'

'I couldn't do that, old thing,' said Brian. 'But I'll demonstrate.'

And he did . . .

Brian puts a noose on Dougal and pulls, throttling him.

'Good method, eh, Dougal?' said Brian.

'It'll revolutionise medicine,' said Dougal.

Florence and Mr MacHenry were still discussing a cure for Zebedee's stiff neck.

'Hammer and chisel?' said Mr MacHenry.

'I don't think so,' said Florence.

'I get the feeling you don't think much of my idea for curing Zebedee,' said Brian.

'*Really?*' said Dougal. 'Whatever gives you that impression?'

'It's just a feeling,' said Brian.

'Give me strength,' said Dougal.

Florence and Mr MacHenry weren't getting much further with their ideas . . .

'Hang him upside down?' said Mr MacHenry.

'I don't think so,' said Florence.

So Dougal and Brian and Florence and Mr MacHenry got together to see what could be done for Zebedee.

'I can't think of anything else,' said Mr MacHenry.

'We could try my rope cure,' said Brian.

'I wish you'd be quiet,' said Dougal.

So Florence decided that she would go and see if Zebedee was any better.

'Yes, go and see if he's any better,' said Mr MacHenry. 'Perhaps it was a temporary affliction.'

So Florence went to see . . . and when she told Zebedee about the various cures everyone had suggested Zebedee decided he'd better do something about it himself – which he did.

'That's better,' he said. 'Time for bed.'

A Weighty Problem

Zebedee asked how Dougal and Brian were getting on.

'I think they like each other *really*,' said Florence.

'*Really?*' said Zebedee.

So Florence went to see if she could find Dougal and Brian . . . and Dougal and Brian were playing together happily.

'Come down!' said Dougal. 'I'm supposed to go up now. This is a see-saw – you're all see and no saw.'

'You're too heavy, Dougal old chum,' said Brian. 'You weigh too much.'

'I'll trouble you not to be personal,' said Dougal, with dignity. 'Are you implying I'm fat? Because if you *are*, there will be *ter*-rouble.'

'Don't be like that,' said Brian. 'Dogs are naturally heavier than snails. It's in the nature of things, old mate.'

'Oh well,' said Dougal. 'If we're going to play see-saw at all, I shall have to make you heavier.'

So Dougal went to find something to make Brian heavier. And Brian went too . . .

Eventually, Dougal and Brian decided to have another go at the see-saw – with a stone on Brian's end to make him heavier.

'Sorry to be such a nuisance, old friend,' said Brian, 'but I'm only little.'

'Excuses, excuses,' said Dougal. 'Nothing but excuses.'

'Sorry,' said Brian.

'It's all right,' said Dougal.

'I can't help it if I'm not big and fat and hairy, can I?' said Brian.

And before Dougal could get his breath back, Florence came along, and Brian told her about him not being heavy enough to play see-saw with Dougal.

'You can't help it,' said Florence.

'Excuses,' said Dougal.

'If we both got on,' said Florence, 'we would be as heavy as Dougal, wouldn't we?'

'Just about,' said Brian.

So that's what they did . . .

'Time for bed,' said Zebedee.

'Now?' said Florence.

'*Now*,' said Zebedee.

'It was fun while it lasted,' said Florence, 'wasn't it?'

Train Trouble

Florence told Zebedee that she wondered if anything exciting would happen today.

'Getting bored?' said Zebedee.

'Oh, no,' said Florence.

But, truth to tell, Florence *was* feeling a bit bored. And she wasn't the only one.

Dougal is in the garden, with a box of matches.

'Playing with fire, Dougal old friend?' said Brian.

'Very funny,' said Dougal.

'I'm *bored*,' said Dougal. 'Why doesn't something *exciting* happen?'

'I'm exciting,' said Brian.

'*No you're not*,' said Dougal. '*No*, you are *not*. I'm going to look for something exciting. Some adventure!'

And he went.

After a short stroll, Dougal eventually comes to a wooden fence.

And Dougal found some adventure – more than he bargained for. Dougal thought he would watch the trains, or perhaps *drive* one, or something. Hee! Hee! But the train had other ideas.

The train sees Dougal and, on a whim, decides to give chase.

'What's going on?' said Mr MacHenry.
'Dougal's in trouble,' said Florence. 'He's being chased by a train.'
'Again?' said Mr MacHenry.

Mr MacHenry chases the Dougal-chasing train. He boards it, stops it, and gets off.

'That's enough of that,' said Mr MacHenry.
'That's enough of that, Dougal,' said Florence.
'What are you getting at me for?' said Dougal.
'That's enough of that,' said Mr MacHenry.
'What are you getting at me for?' said Dougal.

He turns to the train, indignantly.

'You got me into terrible trouble,' said Dougal to the train.
'I'm so sorry,' said the train. 'I got carried away.'
'Try and be more careful,' said Dougal.
'I'll try,' said the train.
'Fun while it lasted,' said Mr MacHenry.
'Had a boring day?' said Zebedee.
'Oh, no!' said Florence.
'Bed then,' said Zebedee.

The Quick Brown Fox

Florence told Zebedee that she had a lot of letters to answer.

'Ask Dougal to help,' said Zebedee. 'He's got a typewriter.'

'Really?' said Florence.

And Dougal *did* have a typewriter.

'Dear Sir, or Madam . . . Hee! Hee! Always like that bit, the quick brown fox jumped over the lazy dog. Oh yes, that'll be the day! Now is the time for all good men to come to the aid of the party. Ho! Ho! What a party! It'll go on all night,' he mumbled.

'Need a secretary?' said Brian. 'Snails make good secretaries.'

'Snails make good snails, that's all,' said Dougal. 'And not many of them do that.'

'What a mood we're in,' said Brian. 'Who are you writing to, old mate?'

'I'm trying to write to Florence,' said Dougal, 'but somehow I keep being interrupted.'

Dougal takes the paper out of the typewriter, then runs around.

'I must do something to keep the garden more *private*,' he said. 'Perhaps I'll speak to Mr MacHenry about a *snail trap*. Ha! Ha!'

'Who for?' said Brian.

'You may well ask,' said Dougal.

'Dear Mr MacHenry, Have you such a thing as a *snail trap* . . . ?' mumbled Dougal, as he typed.

'Lovely day,' said Brian, loudly.

The typewriter breaks and Dougal growls.

'Now look what you've done,' said Dougal. 'Now I'll never be able to finish the letter. Now Florence will *NEVER KNOW* . . .'

'What won't I ever know?' said Florence.

'Don't ask me!' said Dougal, dramatically.

'All right,' said Florence.

And she looked at what Dougal had written.

'The quick brown fox . . .' said Florence.

'That was just practice,' said Dougal. 'The main letter was *COMING LATER* . . .'

'A letter to *me*?' said Florence.

'Yes!' said Dougal.

'Well, you tell me what you wanted to say and I'll type it down,' said Florence, sensibly. 'All right?'

'I suppose so,' said Dougal.

So this is what they did.

Dougal runs around while Florence types.

'Type something for me,' said Zebedee.

'All right,' said Florence.

'Speak slowly and clearly and not too many long words,' said Dougal.

'We're ready,' said Florence and Dougal.

'Time-for-bed,' dictated Zebedee, very slowly and very distinctly.

Push and Pull

Florence told Zebedee that she had a stick of rock but it was too hard to bite.

'Use a saw,' said Zebedee.

'All right,' said Florence.

But sawing sticks of rock was possible only if you had a saw . . . Florence asked Mr MacHenry if he had one.

'Have you a saw?' she said.

'A saw?' said Mr MacHenry.

'A saw,' said Florence.

'See what I can do,' said Mr MacHenry, and he was gone.

I wonder where Dougal is? thought Florence.

And by a strange coincidence Dougal and Brian were using a saw. At least, Dougal was trying to teach Brian how to use a saw . . .

'I push and you pull!' said Dougal. 'And then *you* push and *I* pull! Can't you understand?'

'No,' said Brian.

'How can you be so stupid?' said Dougal.

'It takes practice,' said Brian.

Give me strength, thought Dougal. 'Now listen – you PULL!'

'I pull?' said Brian.

'You pull!' said Dougal.

They try again.

'You pushed! You pushed!' screamed Dougal.

'I thought you said push,' said Brian, giggling.

'I believe you are trying to exasperate me,' said Dougal, with dignity.

'I wouldn't do that, Dougal old mate,' said Brian, giggling.

I can see no *reason* for snails, thought Dougal.

And Mr MacHenry arrived, and explained to Dougal about Florence and the hard stick of rock and he tried out his special saw, which worked very well.

'Works very well,' said Mr MacHenry, with satisfaction.

'That snail would get it wrong, I'll bet,' said Dougal, darkly.

Mr MacHenry told Florence that she could get her hard stick of rock cut up anytime with his special saw.

'Anytime,' said Mr MacHenry.

'Thank you,' said Florence.

And when Mr MacHenry had gone, Dougal told Florence about Brian and the saw and how Brian would push when he should have pulled.

'I despair of that snail sometimes,' he said. 'I just despair.'

'Time for bed,' said Zebedee suddenly.

Which made Florence jump . . .

A Day at the Races

Dougal is staring at the mirror wearing binoculars and a top hat.

Dougal was getting ready to go to the races.

'Oh, you handsome thing you,' said Dougal. 'You're irresistible, you dog.'

'What are you up to?' said Zebedee.

'Oh, nothing much,' said Dougal, airily. 'I'm just going to the races – someone sent me an invitation. *From the palace*,' he whispered. 'Tell Florence to meet me there, will you?'

'All right,' said Zebedee.

And he told Florence that Dougal wanted her to meet him at the races.

'How exciting!' said Florence.

'I hope so,' said Zebedee.

'Who's racing?' said Florence.

'I'm not sure,' said Zebedee, slowly.

Later, Florence stands expectantly at the fence.

Florence was mystified. She'd never been to the fence in the garden before.

How exciting, she thought.

Dougal was busy making sure everything was in order and Florence was more mystified than ever.

'I'm more mystified than ever,' she said.

'Ah! There you are,' said Dougal.

'Yes, here I am,' said Florence.

'But where *are* we?' she said.

'At the races,' said Dougal. 'Can't you tell?'

'What sort of races?' said Florence.

'*Horse* races,' said Dougal, 'with *horses* and . . . and . . . things like that.'

Just then Ermintrude came along and she said she was going to time the races, and she had a big stopwatch to do it with. The only thing *was*, there didn't seem to be anything much to time.

'Where are all the horses?' said Florence, reasonably.

'Patience,' said Ermintrude.

'Sorry,' said Florence, 'but I thought there were going to be horses and . . . and things like that.'

'Patience,' said Dougal (sounding rather worried).

'Sorry,' said Florence, not at all sure that there would ever be any horses, or things like that.

'They're coming! They're coming!' said Ermintrude.

And Dougal got very excited! 'Come on! Come on!' he shouted.

And Florence looked and looked and looked, until at last . . .

'I've won!' said Brian, looking a little hot and flushed. 'A great victory for snails – snails are the greatest. The greatest!!'

Dougal was astounded.

'You're not a *horse*,' he screamed. 'You're an *imposter*.'

'No, he's a *snail*,' said Florence.

'Who won?' said Zebedee.

'Brian,' said Florence. 'By a distance!'

'Well done that snail,' said Zebedee.

'Well done,' said Florence.

'Perhaps we could put him in the Derby,' said Zebedee.

'He'll make our fortunes,' said Florence happily.

'Better have plenty of sleep then,' said Zebedee. 'Good-night.'

Globe-Trotting

'Hello, Florence,' said Zebedee.

'Hello, Zebedee,' said Florence.

And Florence went to see who she could find . . .

The snail had found Dougal . . . and he had something to tell him.

'I'm going round the world,' said the snail.

'You are going to do *what*?' said Dougal, who couldn't believe what he had heard.

'Going round the world – want to come?' said Brian.

'Not today, thank you,' said Dougal.

Going round the world? thought Dougal. He can't be!

Dougal needs time to think about this, so he goes for a walk. In the garden, he meets Florence.

'Do you know what that snail's up to?' said Dougal.

'No, what?' said Florence.

'Well, he *said* . . .' said Dougal.

'Yes?' said Florence.

'Well, he *said* he was going round the world,' said Dougal.

'Going round the *world*?' said Florence.

'That's what he *said*!' said Dougal. 'Of course I didn't answer him! How could he go round the world? It would take him weeks!'

'He does go quite fast,' said Florence, thoughtfully.

'Not *that* fast,' said Dougal.

Elsewhere Brian is perched, snail-like, on a globe.

'Yoo! Hoo!' said the snail. 'I'm in America! I'm in America! Come and see, Dougal matey!'

Brian mutters to himself and hums.

'Did you hear that?' said Florence. 'Brian says he's in America!'

'He couldn't shout that loud,' said Dougal. 'I don't believe a word of it.'

'Let's go and see,' said Florence.

So they went to see.

'I'm beginning to think snails should be kept out of this garden,' said Dougal, with great dignity.

'Super joke, Dougal, eh?' said the snail.

But Dougal was so put out he didn't see the joke. 'Snails were deceivers ever,' he said, cryptically. 'I shall go to my bed.'

'Great joke, Dougal, eh?' said the snail.

But Dougal took to his bed in a huff.

'I thought it was a good joke, Dougal,' said Florence.

'Ah, youth! Youth!' said Dougal, sadly.

'I think you're very funny too – sometimes,' said Florence.

'That's very kind of you,' said Dougal.

And Florence told Zebedee about Brian going round the world.

'He must be tired then,' said Zebedee. 'So . . .'

'Time for bed?' said Florence.

The Leaf-Eater

Zebedee told Florence that he thought the flowers in the garden probably needed watering, which pleased Florence very much as she liked watering flowers . . . and she said so.

'I like watering flowers,' said Florence.

Dougal is in the garden, looking at the flowers.

Dougal was interested in the flowers too. And *SOMEONE ELSE* was interested too. *VERY* interested.

Brian approaches a flower, interestedly. He slides up the stem, and munches the leaves, humming contentedly.

Florence told Dougal about watering the flowers.

'They have to have water, you know,' said Florence.

'Yes, I do know,' said Dougal. 'I'm very interested in flowers and trees and things.'

And he told Florence there was a particular flower he wanted to show her.

So they went to see it. And what did they find? All the leaves had gone.

SOMEONE HAD EATEN THEM.

'It's him!' said Dougal.

'Who?' said Florence.

'It's him! I know it's *him*!' said Dougal.

'Who?' said Florence.

'You wait till I find him!' said Dougal.

'Who?' said Florence. 'Who? Who . . . ?'

'Who indeed?' said the snail, and he hummed a little song.

Florence and Dougal were still searching for *him* although Florence wasn't too sure who they were looking for.

'Who are we looking for, Dougal?' asked Florence.

'I mention no names,' said Dougal, darkly, 'but he has a shell on his back and he likes *leaves*.' And he left.

'He must mean Brian,' said Florence.

'What about Brian?' said Zebedee.

So Florence told him about the flower, and the leaves being eaten and Dougal being furious. And Zebedee laughed. Which made Florence laugh too.

And Zebedee made everything all right again – as he always did.

'He's hiding from me,' said Dougal.

'Who?' said Florence.

'Yes, who?' said Zebedee.

'Oh, you two!' said Dougal.

And Florence went on with her watering.

She comes across Brian and a sorry-looking flower.

'*This* one needs water,' she said, casually. 'All its leaves seem to have fallen off, poor thing.'

And the snail was ashamed. 'Oh dear,' he said.

'That'll teach him,' hissed Dougal. 'The leaf-eater!'

'Hush, Dougal,' said Florence.

'You've never done anything wrong, I suppose?' said

Zebedee.

'That,' said Dougal, 'is beside the point.'

'It always is,' said Zebedee, 'and it's time for bed.'

Brian has an Idea

Florence told Zebedee that as she hadn't seen Mr Rusty lately she was sending him a present. It was some books to read in case he got lonely.

'That's a nice thought,' said Zebedee.

So Florence went to tell Dougal and she found Dougal was sending a present to Mr Rusty, too.

Everyone, it seemed, had thought of Mr Rusty.

'Won't he be pleased,' said Florence.

'Who will?' said the snail.

'Oh dear, here comes trouble,' said Dougal.

'Hello, little friend,' said the snail.

'I wish you wouldn't call me your little friend,' said Dougal. 'I'm not your little friend.'

'But I like you,' said the snail.

And Florence told the snail about sending presents to Mr Rusty, because they hadn't seen him for a long time. And Dougal asked the snail if he was going to send anything. And the snail said he hadn't got anything to send.

'Typical,' said Dougal.

'But I'll think of something,' said the snail, 'you'll see.'

Then Florence helped Dougal to wrap his present.

'I've got an idea,' said the snail.

The snail goes and comes back.

'I've got an idea,' said the snail.

The snail goes and comes back again.

'I've got an idea,' said the snail. 'I've got an idea.'

'I suppose we'll have to hear it,' said Dougal.

'I've got an idea,' said the snail.

'I understand he's got an idea,' said Dougal.

Florence finished the parcel and she saw Brian doing something very odd.

'I think he's going to send *himself* as a present,' said Florence, laughing, as the snail wrapped himself up.

'Send himself?!' said Dougal. 'Who'd want *him*?'

'Mr Rusty *will* get a surprise!' said Florence.

'A shock, more likely,' said Dougal, and he left.

And Florence was just wondering how to send the parcels when Zebedee arrived.

The self-wrapped snail unwraps himself.

And the snail decided not to go after all.

I knew he wouldn't go, thought Dougal.

'I didn't think you'd go,' said Florence.

'He wouldn't want *me*!' said the snail.

'You can say that again,' said Dougal.

'Is it time for bed?' asked Florence.

'Yes,' said Zebedee.

Brian, the Vegetarian

Mr Rusty and Zebedee are at the barrel organ.

Zebedee told Mr Rusty about Florence and Dougal and the snail sending presents.

'It was a very kind thought,' said Mr Rusty. 'And I thought I'd like to do something for *them*.'

'What?' said Zebedee.

'I'll show you,' said Mr Rusty.

'I'll help you,' said Zebedee.

And this is what Mr Rusty and Zebedee did . . .

In the house things cook themselves and cakes begin to multiply, as magic cakes do.

I hope they like them, thought Mr Rusty.

Dougal comes to the house, looks through the window, and sees the cakes.

Ho! Ho! thought Dougal.

'I *do* hope they like them,' said Mr Rusty.

'You'll see!' said Zebedee.

The children find the cakes, and they tuck in, without further ado.

'They *do* like them,' said Mr Rusty, happily.

In the garden, Dougal spies the snail eating a lettuce.

'I don't know how you can eat that stuff,' said Dougal.

'I'm a vegetarian,' said the snail.

'What's a vegetarian?' said Dougal.

'Someone who doesn't eat meat,' said the snail.

'You mean you don't like bones?!' said Dougal, astonished.

'Certainly not – a disgusting habit,' said the snail. 'Shall we go?'

Florence told Mr Rusty that she had enjoyed the cakes and the others said they had too.

'Did you keep some for Dougal?' asked Zebedee.

And of course they hadn't.

'Oh dear,' said Zebedee.

Dougal told the snail he knew where there was something really good to eat.

They walk up to the window of the house.

'You just look through there,' said Dougal, chortling.

So the snail looked. 'There's nothing there,' he said.

'Too late,' said Dougal, sadly. 'Too late. Too late.'

'Try a bit of lettuce,' said the snail.

'Eugh!' said Dougal. 'Eugh! Eugh! Eugh!'

'Sorry, Dougal,' said Florence, feeling rather full and ready for bed.

Brian goes Skiing

'Isn't it hot?!' said Florence when she met Zebedee.

'Is it?' said Zebedee. 'Soon fix that, you see!'

And he certainly did. There was snow everywhere. And over everything.

'Good morning,' said Florence.

'Very sudden shower,' said the snail.

'I'm sorry, that was my fault,' said Florence.

'Don't apologise – I like it,' said the snail.

The snail meets Dougal, goes round him very fast, then leaves.

'How does that snail manage to go so fast?' said Dougal.

The snail goes by again.

'It's unnatural,' said Dougal.

'Oh, do stop,' said Dougal.

'No, go on,' said Florence.

'Don't encourage him,' said Dougal.

'He's enjoying himself,' said Florence.

The snail glides towards them on his skis.

'I enjoyed that,' said the snail.

'Let me have a go,' said Dougal.
'I'm exhausted,' said the snail.
'I'm not surprised,' said Dougal.
'You have a go then,' said the snail.
'Don't rush me,' said Dougal. 'I have to get ready.'
So they watched while Dougal got ready.

Eventually, Dougal skis with the snail.

'Very good, Dougal,' said Florence.
Zebedee arrived.
'They are skiing,' said Florence.
'So I see,' said Zebedee. 'I hope they're not late for bed.'

A Peaceful Day

Florence told Zebedee that she was going to have a quiet day.

'Good luck,' said Zebedee.

And Florence felt very peaceful. Very peaceful.

Florence walks through the flowers, peacefully.

Very peaceful . . .

Dougal was peaceful too . . . Won't get up yet, he thought.

But have you noticed how people who are *up* can't bear to see people still in bed?

'Good morning, good morning, old friend,' said the snail. 'Time to get up.'

'Go away,' said Dougal.

'All right,' said the snail.

But he didn't go far . . .

He arrives at a drum, and starts drumming, snail-like, with his horns.

And Florence wasn't peaceful any more.

'Everybody up!' said the snail.

Dougal is still in bed, wearing an ice-pack.

I shall do that snail an injury one day, thought

Dougal.

What have I done to deserve it? thought Dougal, shaking at the injustice.

So Florence went to see who was making all the noise.

'Are you enjoying yourself?' asked Florence, nicely.

'Yes, thank you,' said the snail.

'Nice peaceful day, isn't it?' said Florence.

'Lovely,' said the snail.

'Pity to spoil it,' said Florence.

'Oh yes, indeed,' said the snail.

So Florence went to see Dougal.

'Hello, Dougal,' she said.

'Go away,' said Dougal.

Dougal looks up from his bedclothes.

'Oh, sorry,' said Dougal. 'I thought you were *that snail*!' he whispered. 'He does it deliberately, you know.'

And he got up and went away, sighing heavily.

'Had a peaceful day?' asked Zebedee.

'Yes, thank you,' said Florence.

'Time for bed then,' said Zebedee.

'Already?' said Florence.

'It's nearly time for the news,' said Zebedee, 'and you've had enough magic for one day.'